JESUS
Healer of Our
Inner World

JACK WALTERS

Reprinted by   IAM Center 2000
    RR 1   Box 75, New Albany, PA. 18833

Printed in the United States of America

Library of Congress Cataloging-in-Publication Data

Walters, Jack.
    Jesus : healer of our inner world / Jack Walters.
        p.   cm.
    Includes bibliographical references.
    ISBN 0–8245–1528–5 (pbk.)
    1. Pastoral counseling.   2. Jesus Christ—Psychology.   3. Psychotherapy.
4. Spiritual life—Christianity.   5. Spiritual healing.   6. Christianity—
Psychology.   I. Title.
BV4012.2.W35   1995
232'.01'9—dc20   95–19256
                                                                                        CIP

JESUS
Healer of Our
Inner World

To

REBECCA

ANDREW

VALERIE

and

All the lost sheep who have helped me find the way to this
understanding of the Incarnation

Contents

Acknowledgments

In the writing of any book, there are so many people to thank for a multitude of reasons.

First, I would like to thank Sharyn Kolberg for her dedicated assistance in editing this book and her incredible skill in distilling it into readable text while not losing one iota of my intended meaning. To her, I owe my profoundest thanks and gratitude.

Without the help and encouragement of Don Kraus, the reading of this book as a published work might not have been possible. It was his encouragement and professional advice that helped get this work into publishable form and then his kind references to publishers that brought the book into reality.

I would like to thank my colleague at IAM Counseling and Retreat Center, Fred Strugatz, for his constant encouragement, support and review of this work as it has evolved throughout the years. Also, the fact that he is of the Jewish tradition, and that he has been discovering its rich spiritual heritage, has helped me understand better who Jesus was in the context of being a Jew; how it was the root of what he taught and represented; and how it determined the way in which he related to the religious leaders and common people.

I also need to thank Gila Dunn, the administrative assistant at the Center, for her hard work in entering the endless corrections of the manuscript into the word processor, transferring information from disk to disk, and for keeping track of all the necessary communications with all the people this kind of work involves.

I would also like to thank Thelma Dixon-Murphy, a long-time friend, former teacher and now supervisor, and Sheffa Gold, a new friend and teacher. Both reflected on and challenged old and/or presumptive ways of expressing religious ideas that required me to dig a little deeper to articulate better the meaning of those expressions.

Finally, I would like to thank all those who have attended workshops I have given on this subject, as well as those who have read the various editions of the manuscript over the years. Their questions, comments, and challenges have been most helpful to me to bring this work to its present place.

∞Introduction∞
Jesus and the Unconsciousness

THE HUMAN CONDITION

Some years ago, at a workshop I was conducting, a woman asked me a question. I have never forgotten the ensuing dialogue between us. I had just finished talking about the fundamental goodness and worthiness of every human being, based on the affirmation in Genesis, chapter one, that we have been created in the image and likeness of God.

Joan (all names in this book have been changed to safeguard confidentiality) understood me intellectually, and agreed with me—in theory. But when she considered Jesus' sacrifice, she felt a profound sense of unworthiness. As a result, she experienced an enormous gulf between her Self and God.

The following dialogue puts her conflict into bold relief:

Joan: Suppose I met Jesus. I would say, "Lord, I am so glad to see you. But I feel so unworthy of you. There is such a difference between You and me."

Jack: What would you do if Jesus said back to you, "But, Joan, why do you feel so unworthy of me?"

Joan: Because I've never lived up to the vision of my Self.

Jack (still speaking as Jesus): What is that vision of your Self that stands between you and me?

Joan: I believe it is because I am human.

Jack (as Jesus): Yet I am human also. I am a human being, and I am here with you now in your time and space. So what is this unworthiness you speak of?

Joan: It is my inconstancy, my sloth.

Jack (as Jesus): But I see beyond your inconstancy and sloth. I love you for who you are.

Joan: It's hard for me to accept that.

These profound feelings of guilt and shame not only tore Joan apart from the inside, but they imposed an unbridgeable chasm between her Self and God (and between her Self and others in her life as well). Even as I was trying to counter this internal view of her Self, she exclaimed, "I hear what you're saying, but these feelings really seem to rule me. I feel so guilty and ashamed!"

At another point in our dialogue, I asked Joan what she had in fact done to bring about her guilt and shame. She could not identify anything other than *the fact that she existed*.

I pointed out to her that when she succumbed to that profound sense of unworthiness, she was accepting two inner assumptions about her Self. The first was that she had to *do* something to merit God's free gift of life. The second was that she had to do something *even before she existed* to merit this gift.

Further, because her mere existence generated such terrible feelings of guilt and shame, she desperately searched for forgiveness for a sin she had committed, but could not identify. No matter how strenuously she sought that forgiveness, and no matter what she did in penance for that "sin," she could never relieve her Self of the guilt and shame that gripped her. She could not accept or assimilate the fact that her creation was God's loving act, and out of that act flowed her own intrinsic goodness and worth. Her guilt and shame erected a seemingly insurmountable wall between her Self and God.

In our dialogue, two distinct theologies emerged. Hers was one of shame and guilt as she stood before God. Mine was a theology of fundamental goodness, intrinsic to the creation of our being, coming from the love and fullness of God as recounted in Genesis 1. These two theologies are diametrically opposed and incompatible with one another. These two theologies are often in conflict within the Judeo-Christian tradition and was the point of contention between Jesus and the mainstream Judaism of his day.

I have come to realize that this conflict and contradiction is the underlying problem of *every person* with whom I have worked as a pastoral counselor. It was the pervasiveness and constancy of this dynamic that drew me to explore the connection between our psychological process and who we are as spiritual beings.

PSYCHOTHERAPY AS A SPIRITUAL PROCESS

In my view, the goal of the psychotherapeutic process is to direct the person to an examination of his or her inner world in order to discover and resolve the inner turmoil that blemishes and hides the intrinsic goodness of his or her spiritual identity. As the person proceeds in that task and as the darkness that blankets the soul begins to lift, the person's real spiritual identity and awareness becomes more apparent.

Although the psychotherapeutic process is usually regarded as a secular, non-spiritual enterprise, I believe quite the opposite is true. As a matter of fact, I believe one of the current problems in psychotherapy is the failure to recognize and admit the essentially spiritual character of the process.

To me, spirituality is the journey each of us takes to come to terms with who we are within our Selves and in relation to the cosmos. The spiritual task that faces each of us is to find the unique way in which our spiritual awareness and identity best expresses itself. As we come to terms with our own spiritual identity, we open up our Selves to the spiritual dimension of others in the world as well.

When we are prevented by deep currents within us that block us from accepting our own spiritual identity, our ability to accept and allow that to grow in others is severely hampered. In addition, our view, understanding and experience of God are distorted as well.

Therefore, I see psychotherapy as a spiritual process by which human beings bring their unique qualities of Self-consciousness to full flower.

MYTHOLOGY AND THE PSYCHOLOGICAL PROCESS

According to author, philosopher, and theologian Joseph Campbell, the mythology of any culture is its attempt to express the journey each must take in order to attain human fulfillment. Every mythology, religious or secular, is replete with stories of heroes and heroines who must pass through an underworld and so be transformed into a new life that transcends the old.

One interpretation of this underworld is that it represents the realm of the unconscious. In that realm, these heroic figures point the way for all of us, in terms of the path we are to follow if we are to be released from the inner powers that keep our souls shrouded in darkness.

Anthropological and literary studies show that most (if not all) cultures possess mythologies that grapple with these issues of the unconscious. In our industrialized, secular society, movies such as Spielberg's *Star Wars* and *Poltergeist* are contemporary attempts to wrestle with these inner realities of light and darkness that are a part of the communal, human consciousness.

Story telling is but one of the vehicles by which human beings have attempted to work out the conflicts that emerge from our personal and collective unconscious. In some cultures there are those who live out the mythology of their people. Native North Americans have individuals identified as shamans, who often go through intense experiences of enlightenment in which the "inner truth" is revealed. In some African cultures, shamans assist people who have external manifestations of internal conflicts (psychosomatic illnesses) to enter into their unconscious realm through ritual experience so that the inner turmoil can be resolved and their illness healed.

In these cultures, the shaman is the hero who confronts the unconscious content of the psyche by entering into that realm herself. (One word on a technical issue: in order to avoid the gender bias in this book by constantly using "he" in stories and examples—it's very awkward to use "he/she" and "him or her" throughout—I opted to use "he" in some examples, and "she" in others. I will also use this device in reference to God, since God is neither male nor female, but has attributes that, to us, represent the masculine and feminine.) As a result of that confrontation, a shaman becomes a beacon or guide for the individual to travel through that dark realm herself.

Like shamans in other cultures, the therapist is one who, through her own spiritual journey, has wrestled with her own unconscious conflicts and can now be a guide for others who are confronted with the intrusion of unresolved unconscious conflicts. What pastoral psychotherapy does is explore with the individual how the inner world of the human unconscious impacts on his relationship with himself and others, including God. The discipline grapples with how the religious tradition and its own mythology and ritual address the issues of the unconscious that block human consciousness from reaching its fullest potential, and how the religious tradition can help people come to a resolution of the internal conflicts that are borne within them.

Religion and psychotherapy can work in tandem, as many of their goals are similar. Both are there to assist the individual to come to terms with who he is. They can and should be friends who work together, enriching the existences of those who participate in their processes.

THE JESUS MYTH

Although each person has his own personal mythology that he must articulate if he is to come to terms with his own internal conflicts, there are myths that come out of the collective awareness of the unconscious that express in broader terms what that inner journey is all about.

There are a multitude of references to the conflict between the powers of darkness and light in the Jesus myth as it is articulated in Scripture.

Jesus, as a heroic figure, addresses the power of the underworld of our unconscious. He holds out a beacon to us so that we might reconstruct our own personal mythology with a new inner mythology in which we are re-created in the image and likeness of God.

To grasp the meaning of the Jesus myth, it must be understood that it does not begin with the Gospel stories. Rather, it starts at the very opening of the total Judeo-Christian mythological cycle, the Genesis story. (The term Judeo-Christian means there can be no understanding of Jesus as Messiah without understanding the mythology of the Chosen People of Israel.) The meaning of Jesus cannot in any way be understood outside of the context of the totality of that cycle. The Judeo-Christian mythology is a journey along the curved line of a circle. The point at which we begin will be the point at which we end; our point of departure will be the first chapter of Genesis.

In chapter one of Genesis, humankind is created in the image and likeness of God, and regarded by God as very good. By the end of chapter three of that same book that goodness is despoiled. This change from "goodness" to "badness" sets up an apparent contradiction which produces tension and conflict within the entire mythology. Within the Christian framework, this tension and conflict is the energy that drives the mythology through its cyclical course to its resolution in and through the Jesus myth.

THE DEMONIC WITHIN OUR PSYCHE

In his book *People of the Lie* Scott Peck ponders whether Satan exists as the personification of evil. Challenging the reader not to dismiss the concept as medievalist-religious hogwash, Peck describes his presence at, participation in and observations of exorcisms involving individuals whom he considers to be possessed of demonic, evil forces. I also ask you, the reader, not to dismiss the concept of Satan as merely a pious construction to frighten people into a childish dependency on religion. My understanding of the Satanic power, however, is different from Peck's.

Children are developmentally empowered around the age of two to construct internal images of their "important others." Through these internalized images, they develop ways of avoiding behavior that we understand will jeopardize their connection with the all-important Others (mother, father, and so on). I call these internalized images, who, as we will see, exist as very active personas within our psyches, the Inner Other.

When we leave childhood, we no longer need these internalized images. But they continue to exist within our psyche anyway. It is in the transition from childhood to adulthood that the Inner Other is transformed from a blessing to a curse. Essentially, the Inner Other identifies the outside world as dangerous, and promises the person that if he listens to its directions, it will save him from the danger and give him life.

During my twenty years of clinical experience I have witnessed the power the Inner Other has over people's souls and the tricks it practices on them to keep them in its slavery. The force Peck describes seems to me to be the ultimate extreme of a psychological entity that is a reality for all of us. I have not engaged, nor am I eager to engage, in exorcisms of the kind Peck describes in order to find out if that archetypal "Satan" does roam the world plundering vulnerable souls. I know, however, that the "Satanic" force I *do* encounter in my daily work as a psychotherapist is powerful enough for me to respect that it exists. I further believe that, since it is an entity within the psyche of every human being, this experience is something common to us all.

The premise of this work, then, is that the Inner Other is the demonic force found in each of us that attempts to and often does take over our identities, becoming our master. I have no doubt that each one of us has one or more personal demons, with identities all their own. In addition, not only do they exist within us, but we have and maintain very intense psychological and emotional relationships with them.

FROM UN-WHOLENESS TO HOLINESS

Certainly, Jesus' call is to holiness. In Webster's *New World Dictionary*, holiness is defined as the quality or state of being holy. The word comes from the Anglo-Saxon word "hal" meaning sound or whole. To exist in a holy state, then, means to be in soundness and wholeness.

This book will examine how we, as humans, become "un-whole" and "fractured" as a part of the growing up process. As a result, we become wholenesses divided within our Selves. We are divided into disconnected entities within our Selves that are often at war with each other. As long as it remains unaddressed, this state of unholiness has a profound impact on who we are during adulthood.

This book will explore how the Jesus myth addresses this inner split and the inner political arrangement that is the result of the fractured parts of the Self and the activity of the Inner Other.

Like all myths, the Jesus myth articulates the struggle between the powers of darkness and of light. The Inner Other is the demon force, the power of darkness of the Gospel stories. This inner demon, created by each one of us, maintains the belief that we are worthless as individuals and as a species. Having seduced us into that mindset, the Inner Other then seduces us to worship it by convincing us that it is necessary for our survival. But, in fact, the life it promises us is a shroud that engulfs us in spiritual death.

Understanding this, I will explore how Jesus helps and requires us to relinquish our connection to the false promises of the Inner Other. I will then contemplate how the Word, Jesus, helps us achieve our independence from the power of darkness within by calling us to follow the truth of our birthright, of being created in the image and likeness of God. We will see how, by claiming the real truth of the Self that heretofore has been hidden from us by this demonic force of the Inner Other, we are enabled to heal the unholiness of our soul and return to a soundness of spirit that was intended for us by our Creator God.

Through this work, then, I will explore the struggle we all have with this internal demonic force and how the Jesus myth addresses this, the deepest of spiritual struggles. Beginning with the Garden myth, I will show how a myth such as this defines the point of departure of the human struggle and how Jesus' life, passion, death and resurrection bring that cycle to completion.

PART I

The Original Sin

∞ 1 ∞

I Am Who Am

IN THE IMAGE OF GOD

*I*n the beginning, God said, "Let us make humankind in our image, after our likeness . . . " So God created humans in God's own image and likeness, and God blessed them and "behold, it was very good."
In these few lines of the Genesis story (1:26–31), we have the declaration of faith of the Judeo-Christian tradition. God is not only a God who can bring being out of nothingness, but this God also creates a being in Her own image and likeness. This God, then, has a very personal and intimate relationship with Her special creation, humankind.

To be created in the image and likeness of the Creator is quite a distinction, but what does it really mean? The answer to this question comes a bit later, in Exodus (3:13–14), when God appears to Moses in the form of a burning bush that is not consumed in the flame. In the course of their interchange Moses asks, "If I go to the people of Israel and tell them that the God of our fathers has sent me, what shall I tell them is your name?" The Voice says, "I am who I am" (YHWH [In some traditions, to utter the name of God is presumptuous because that would "contain" God, and God cannot be contained. Therefore, we eliminate the vowels, which doesn't contain or limit God]). "Tell them I AM has sent me to you."

Since we, as humans, were created in God's image and likeness, we have also inherited the qualities of Her IAM-ness. My own understanding of what this IAM-ness means came first when I was a young boy in Buffalo, New York.

THE EXPERIENCE OF IAM-NESS

It was Easter Sunday morning and I was sitting on the back steps of our home. I was four years old and I was thoroughly enjoying this warmer-than-usual

Spring day. The sky was a translucent robin's-egg blue. The clouds billowed into fantastic pictures of animals and people. Somewhere in the background there was the drone of a single engine plane. In the far right-hand corner of the yard was a pussy willow in bloom that had attracted to it hundreds of buzzing bees.

I turned my head and caught a glimpse of the sun. It shone so gold it was almost silver. It gleamed magnificently and I saw its beam jut through the clouds across the universe. I had to squint.

At that moment I noticed a curious protrusion beneath my eyes. Amazing! It was my nose! Of course, I knew it was there; I had seen it many times before in the mirror. I had touched it many times. But this time my awareness of it was very different. I realized I was seeing it from a very special perspective, as only *I* could see it! And then I realized an incredible fact: of all the people in the world—no, the universe—only I could see my nose this way. It was I who was looking out of those windows, my eyes, onto the world. No one else could see out of my windows or see my nose as I did; no one else could see my nose from my side!

For the first time in my life I was aware of my Self: I-AM-WHO-I-AM. I am an "I." I am a "yahweh," created, but a yahweh nevertheless.

THE IAM QUALITIES

From that initial insight, another quickly followed. I realized for the first time in my existence that I was the only person in the world who could peer at the world from my own unique perspective. No one else could see what I saw from my point of view. Out of that realization I understood that *I* was the only me there was in the entire world, the entire universe.

The discovery I made that day eventually led me to recognize other qualities included in my own IAM-ness. I discovered my radical separateness from others: I possess an inner existence within the parameters of my body, and it is mine alone; that inner existence separates me from the rest of the world. I have my identity and you have yours; we are not the same.

Furthermore, within these parameters, my identity is inviolable. Emanating from deep within comes my sense of who I am. Despite any onslaughts from without, no one (including myself) can totally obliterate that inner existence. My sense of my IAM-ness remains intact. No matter how hard someone might try to tell me who I am, what I should want, need, think, know or feel, my integrity and identity from within are maintained. Deep inside, that inner sense, that integrity remains and even I cannot change it.

Once I discovered that inner place of integrity, I also became aware that I am the only one "in charge" of my IAM-ness. No matter how I might try to become what I think others want me to be, deep inside, where that place of integrity rests, I am empowered to be who I AM.

Over the years, I have also discovered that my IAM-ness is timeless. That "I" which became Self-aware so many years ago sitting on those steps is the very same "I" who sits here reflecting and writing at this moment. Yes, changes have occurred: opinions have been formulated, rejected and reformulated over the years; my knowledge has increased; my sensations and perceptions of the world have altered from moment to moment. The central awareness of my Self, however, has remained unaltered, unchanged and ever-in-the-present. I AM WHO I AM. No one event, nor the passage of time itself, ever changes or alters that single truth.

Finally, if I allow myself to experience all of the above qualities, I then have an experience of solidity, of knowing that I am not a vacuum, empty. Rather, I experience my Self as being full and substantial in my IAM-ness.

In that moment of clarity some fifty years ago, and through these years of reflection upon it, I believe that I have recognized and defined the seven qualities of IAM-ness that are, in each of us, in the image and likeness of God:

1. The fact of my IAM-ness.
2. The uniqueness of the IAM.
3. The separateness or autonomy of the IAM.
4. The integrity of the IAM.
5. The inner empowerment of the IAM.
6. The timelessness of the IAM.
7. The sense of inner substance as a person in the experience of these other qualities.

The central quality, then, of being created in the image and likeness of the YHWH lies in the awareness of the Self—I AM WHO I AM or I AM WHO AM. Contained in that Self-awareness are these other six qualities of uniqueness, autonomy, integrity, and its radical inviolability, timelessness, and the inner substantiality of the "I." And all of these attributes are our inheritance from our creation in the image of God.

BEING IN THE IAM

When I am centered in all seven aspects of IAM-ness, I experience my Self as a mirror of God's image and likeness; therefore I open my Self to a new closeness with God. I prepare my Self to communicate with God without words, concepts or thoughts. By being in my created I-AM-WHO-AM-ness, I ready my Self to touch and be touched by the Uncreated I-AM-WHO-AM. If I open my Self to being my own I-AM-WHO-AM, I set the stage for knowing God through that I-AM-WHO-AM-ness. When I am in the pure I-AM-WHO-AM state of being, YHWH, the Uncreated IAM, passes over, in, and through me so that I, as a Self-aware being, am surrounded, engulfed, and infinitely touched by *the* uncreated Self-Aware Being.

It is for this purpose that each human person was created—to live in perfect harmony, communication and intimacy with God the Creator and with his or her Self.

∞2∞

The Fall from Grace

THE DIMMING OF THE GIFT

Unfortunately for us, the pure state of I-AM-WHO-AM-ness (and the six IAM qualities that flow out of it) does not remain pure and readily available to us. Instead, it appears muddied and sullied by deep currents of guilt, anxiety, worthlessness, and shame that abide within most of us.

Through my work as a pastoral psychotherapist, I have come to realize that these feelings, and the negative behavior and attitudes they generate, stem from the human developmental process. This chapter will explore some of the ways in which our childhood struggles towards autonomy and independence can leave us with a profound, pervasive sense of guilt and shame about our existence.

I will also examine the Creation myth (using the term myth to mean a traditional story serving to explain the deeper meaning of some aspect of human reality) as found in Genesis. Here, the original sense of the goodness of human creation sketched in chapter one, when God first creates humankind, is darkened by chapter three, when Adam and Eve have eaten from the tree of knowledge.

In this myth, the original innocence of Adam and Eve has become overshadowed by a profound sense of guilt and shame as they stand before God. Adam and Eve have disobeyed the word, the prohibition of God, their creator and nurturer. Because they have done so, they incur the wrath of God, who is their parent, and are summarily banished from the paradise of Eden. This was a place where all they needed was provided without asking; now they must "toil after their sustenance."

We will therefore explore the story of Adam and Eve and their "expulsion" from the Garden of Eden as the connection between the human psychological condition and the theological explanation of it.

A PSYCHOLOGY OF GUILT AND SHAME

Every adult knows that growing up is filled with challenges, conflicts, and ambiguities. There are times when these conflicts become so great they cause us to dis-integrate our Selves, to split off the parts of our Selves that we think are "bad." This splitting of the Self creates a hole in the soul, and results in a deep sense of inner personal emptiness and shame.

Like any other feeling, though, shame has its appropriate place. When, in reality, we have done something that radically transgresses our own sense of values, we experience our Selves as devalued in our own eyes—that is, we feel shame. The proper function of that feeling is to alert us to that transgression so that we will not violate our sense of values in the same way again.

However, many of us experience what John Bradshaw, in his book *Healing the Shame that Binds Us*, calls toxic shame. Toxic shame is a chronic state of the devaluation of the Self which evolves out of a primal perception that there is something essentially "wrong with me." When this toxic feeling permeates the awareness of who I am, I experience my Self with the hole in the soul referred to above.

Furthermore, toxic guilt is a chronic belief that if anything goes wrong between you and me—"it is always my fault."

Where do toxic shame and guilt come from? To understand their source, we need to turn to the human developmental process.

CHILD WATCHING

All children begin as passive participants in the world. When they are cold, hungry, wet, or otherwise uncomfortable, the world comes to them and satisfies their needs. Infants seem quite delighted with this arrangement. As long as they are comfortable, they are content to be where they are.

As babies begin to grow and their motor skills increase, they are not so content to remain where they have been put. At the same time, they are learning to formulate sounds and words, and eventually to give meaning to these words. Being attended to then begins to seem almost a nuisance; what becomes most important is exploration. As soon as a toddler finds something new, he wants to handle it, push it, climb it, shove it, drop it. The environment is no longer space that wraps itself around him; it is something through which the child catapults himself.

Such a child is coming into Self-awareness. Although not consciously aware of it, he is learning through discovery: this is *my* hand holding this round thing; *I* can make this thing move; when I make it move, it moves away from me, *it is not part of me.*

While all this is going on, there are also significant changes occurring in the child's interpersonal environment. Suddenly, in the middle of the most delightful explorations, adults are saying, "NO!" or "You can't do that!" or "Don't put that in your mouth!" This is when the child's personal Garden of Eden comes to an end.

I distinctly remember one child going through this process. Judith was about eighteen months old when she, her parents, myself, and several other adults were celebrating Christmas in my new home, which was only partially completed. This was definitely not a "child-proof" environment. Our attention was constantly focused on where Judith was and what she was doing.

For her, this was a wonderland. For the adults, it was a nightmare. Every time one of us stopped Judith from doing something that would be harmful to her, she would protest—loud and long. Gradually, wonderland lost some of its luster.

As Judith catapulted herself through this space, she was undergoing a significant developmental process: as she explored all the objects contained within that space, she was beginning to experience her Self. She was on her way to that moment of Self-awareness which engulfed me that Easter morning so long ago. But for her, as for me and for everyone else, the journey toward that moment is not without trial, struggle and conflict.

Each time one of us intervened in her wonderful adventure, we faced a struggle with Judith. And each intervention also caused a struggle *within* Judith. Each interruption meant, to her, that she was being thwarted from an experience that would bring her closer to the Self-aware moment, the moment of identity within her Self and autonomy from others.

It is easy to understand, then, how a child comes to believe that Self-knowledge is "wrong." Judith could not understand, as she headed for a dangerous stairwell, that we grabbed her for her own protection. All she knew was that the activity that fulfilled the instinctual need for arriving at Self-awareness was being stopped by the "all-powerful others." Thus, at a very primal level, she (and all children) experience a conflict, a forbiddenness around their quest for Self-discovery, mastery of the environment, and autonomy from others.

SAYING NO

There comes a time in every child's development when he or she discovers the word "no" and seems compelled to use it incessantly. Although this is an exasperating and often difficult time for her caretakers, the "terrible twos" are a psychological necessity for the child. The word "no" is very powerful. It brings the child to the radical discovery that he is a being separate from others, and that he has some internal powers over his Self and others. The word "no" introduces the child to the psychological reality of autonomy from his or her parenting figures.

This introduction to autonomy, however, is not without some degree of ambivalence. Take this scenario for example: Mrs. Smith is on a long-distance call to her sister in Seattle. Susie, Mrs. Smith's two-and-a-half-year-old daughter, is sitting on the kitchen floor banging pots with a wooden spoon. Susie thinks she is making beautiful music. Mrs. Smith thinks Susie is making a lot of noise, and interrupting her conversation. When Mrs. Smith asks Susie to stop, her response is a very firm "NO!" She is asked to stop twice more, and each time responds with an emphatic "NO!" Finally, Mrs. Smith removes the pots and spoon and sends Susie to her room.

Susie is playing with the word "no" in an earnest attempt to test her physical and psychological boundaries. Because she is still in the learning process, she has just stepped over the line. Mrs. Smith is punishing Susie for interrupting her conversation. But in Susie's mind, she is being punished for attempting to achieve autonomy and identity.

When we multiply this typical child-parent interaction by the number of such interactions each day, times the days, weeks and years, times the number of parental figures involved, we can begin to understand how a child's striving for singular, unique identity and autonomy is fraught with danger and conflict.

Since all children go through some degree of conflict around their pursuit of autonomy, it is understandable that we all leave childhood with some degree of ambivalence and disturbance about our Selves in autonomy. It is further understandable how the myth of Eve and Adam evolved as humankind's attempt to come to both religious and psychological terms with this conflict.

A Theology of Guilt and Shame

What exactly happened when Adam and Eve ate of the tree of knowledge?

First, Adam and Eve became aware of their Selves, of each other, and of their nakedness. They covered themselves with fig leaves. They heard God walking around in the Garden and they hid behind some bushes, ashamed to appear naked before Him. The fact that they realized their nakedness, and were ashamed of it, implies that they had gained a sense of Self-awareness.

They also became aware of good and evil, right and wrong. When that happened, they realized they were separate and autonomous from others, because right and wrong exist in terms of what each person does or does not do to another. If I am alone, by my Self, there is not much I can do to get into trouble against my Self. However, once I begin to interact with others, right and wrong, good and evil become real issues.

So eating from the tree of knowledge brought with it Self-awareness: the knowledge that I AM WHO I AM, with a sense of identity about my Self. And, eating the fruit also brought with it the sense of separateness from others, the internal awareness of autonomy.

Yet, as we saw in the previous chapter, these are two traits that are intrinsic to the gift of IAM-ness, the gift of being created in the image and likeness of God. Somewhere along the line, knowing who I am within my Self, and knowing who you are as separate from me, has been deemed a sin, a terrible act of ingratitude and rebellion against the good God who had the generosity to bring me into being and to provide everything for me that I could ever want.

Having "rebelled" and eaten of the forbidden fruit, Adam and Eve claim their identity and autonomy; they demonstrate that they have minds of their own. In that, they are god-like: they have an internal sense of their own identities as well as inner empowerment, and they know and understand right from wrong.

What is so wrong about that? Weren't Adam and Eve god-like to begin with—created in Her image and likeness? It seems then, that there is a profound contradiction between chapters one and three of the Genesis story.

EXPLAINING THE SIN

The Garden myth is an attempt to make some sense out of a universal experience: our instinctual striving for personal identity, for integrity and empowerment within our Selves, and for autonomy from others—and the shame and guilt we experience when we strive toward these things. Adam and Eve are not just simple characters in a story—they are complex humans with complex human psychological conflicts. The Garden myth represents the origin of the human psychological struggle in the language of religious mythology.

We, as children, experience our Selves as being "bad" when we strive after our Selves in autonomy. We begin the knowledge of our Selves as separate individuals by disobeying our god-like parents, just as Adam and Eve disobeyed God. When we do so, we become aware of our Selves and our actions. We are aware we have disobeyed; we give up our "favored nation" status as we continue in the struggle for Self-awareness and autonomy. We feel guilt and shame at the same time we feel growth and accomplishment. The tension all children experience with their parental figures while striving toward identity and autonomy is the same tension we find in the Garden myth.

This brings us back to the original contradiction. Adam and Eve were created in the image and likeness of God; as we have seen, to be in that image is to be Self-aware, and to be rooted in our own identity. But we have also seen that to be rooted in our own identity, we must realize and act on our autonomy from others.

In chapter three of Genesis, though, we find that the very conditions of Self-awareness and autonomy that are required to be in the image and likeness of God have become forbidden, and have become a horrible sin against the Parent-God. For this sin, a terrible punishment is levied against Adam and Eve: Woman is to bear the intense and dangerous pain of childbirth, and is to be submissive to her husband. Man is to toil with the rebellious earth, stubborn with thorns and thistles; he will no longer have the delicate fruits of the garden to eat, but instead will have fibrous wild plants. And both Man and Woman will suffer death.

ADAM AND EVE IS OUR NAME

Just as it had for Adam and Eve, becoming Self-aware and independent has deep ramifications for each of us. Once a child understands what she wants and has the power to go after it, she also discovers that the world is no longer organized around her every desire. In fact, the outside world often prohibits her from getting her way. The result is that the child enters into a power conflict with her parental figures to see just how far she can extend her boundaries.

Once I heard my friend's daughter Judith say to her father, who was buttoning up her coat, "No! No! Me do! Me do!" Although the task took a lot longer for Judith to accomplish, it was important for her own psychological and spiritual well-being that she do it herself. In this particular case, there was no reason Judith should not try and button her own coat. But if there had been a real need for speed (a train to catch, an emergency situation), there would have been a terrific power struggle between Judith and her father.

On one hand, the child is pushed by her instinct to assert her autonomy. On the other hand, the parent is working within a strict time frame.

When these two agendas clash, the child is faced with the parent's anger and frustration, which mounts as the power struggle intensifies.

Each child becomes an Adam or Eve who inevitably finds his or her Self in conflict and competition with the all-powerful, all-knowing, always-present god-like parental figure. When this struggle occurs, it is experienced by the child as wrong, bad, and shameful.

The child is ashamed because she is disrupting the order of love as she has so far understood it. Up until now, love has meant total care and protection. Now the child is rejecting some of that care and protection, and believes she is rejecting some of that love as well.

The thought process goes like this: "If I challenge and reject the authority of my parent (god) over me, I reject the love of that parent (god) as well. That means that I reject the very well-spring of my being. There must be something wrong with me to reject this kind of love. I am ashamed of my Self."

Of course, young children do not actually think these coherent thoughts. But the content is there in the dim awareness of the child's mind. It is precisely because these thoughts are not clearly articulated that they fester, and emerge later in adulthood. These beliefs about the Self, then, to varying degrees, eat away at the life force of the individual.

A Theology of the Unconscious

In theological terms, the wrath of God is visited upon us through the expulsion from Eden, because we have refused the god-love. We are being punished by having to experience all the pain and suffering of life. In psychological terms, the wrath of God is the guilt and shame we all experience as part of the human condition. All of us live with some degree of toxic shame and guilt. As a therapist, I work with people who are experiencing extreme states of guilt and shame, depression and anxiety. It is precisely these extreme states, however, that help us to better analyze and understand the process and nature of the conflicts of the "inner world" we each possess; those who are in the greatest pain often give us the greatest insights.

This inner world and internal conflict is not a modern phenomenon. In Rom. 7:13–20, Paul articulates his inner conflicts when he talks about sin working within him. He proclaims that he does not understand his own actions. He does things he does not want to do, he says, and even though he wills himself to "do the right thing," he does not do it. Paul calls this the power of sin that overtakes him.

I call it the unconscious. No matter what it is called it is the same human reality. And it is this human reality, this creation of an inner world, this fracturing of the Self into disparate parts that is the power of sin. In this inner world of the fractured Self, we create an internal image of the powerful "parent" who is to be pleased. This internal image becomes what I call the Inner Other. It is the dynamic interaction between the Inner Other and the disparate parts of the Self that creates the true sin in our lives. The pureness of who we are in the created image and like-ness of God is badly distorted. *This is what sin really is: that we are miss-ing the mark; we are not achieving what God intends for us—to love and respect the beauty of our own participation in the Being of God, and to love and respect that in others as well.*

Whether one calls it the power of sin, as Paul did, or the power of the unresolved conflicts in the unconscious, as it is known in modern psy-chotherapy, it all belongs to the universal human experience. Whether we understand our Selves from a psychological or theological point of view, the ultimate truth about who we are as human beings rests in who we are in our IAM-ness. The disciplines of psychology and theology are not radically disparate systems of thought. Rather, each takes the same phe-nomenon, the IAM-ness of the human person, and examines and illu-minates the human experience in its own special way. In so doing, each adds to the total picture of what is to be human.

THE PSYCHOLOGY OF ADAM AND EVE

It is important to combine these two perspectives in order to understand the Garden myth. This story tries to makes sense out of the human con-dition and the circumstances of existence. It says: humans suffer greatly here on earth. We have war and famine and crime and death. We *must* have done something wrong to deserve this punishment.

There are definite parallels between this explanation and themes I hear daily in my work as a pastoral psychotherapist: "I feel such pain (guilt, shame, loneliness, anxiety, fear, rage, and the like); there must be something wrong with me. I must have done something to deserve this." Most people with whom I work perceive the pain and the circumstances of the life in which they find themselves as punishment for their "low value" as a person.

The belief that "there must be something wrong with me because of the pain I feel" originates in childhood. The hallmark of a child's think-ing is its magical egocentricity. There is a misplaced sense of cause and effect which results in toxic guilt: "I was a bad boy. That's why Daddy left us.

It's my fault." Or, "I was angry with my little sister and she got hit by a car. It was my fault." Or, it results in toxic shame: "I feel so bad about Daddy leaving. Nobody understands how bad I feel. I'm not even worth being understood. I must be no good."

Magical thinking is assigned to events that have no relationship to each other beyond the fact that they happened concurrently. The little girl who blames her Self for her sister's accident because she was angry with her at the time, joins these two events (anger plus accident) as a cause and effect.

A child has no way to understand that his or her actions or emotions had nothing to do with the events that followed. At this stage of development, there are no boundaries between what we do, and what happens to us and others around us. We take the burden of the things that happen onto our Selves, and perceive our Selves as flawed from within.

This kind of thinking does not always involve traumatic events. An example of a "normal" trauma would be the birth of a second child into a family. To onlookers, there may not be much apparent jealousy. The older child, however, may be experiencing tremendous rage against her sibling and her parents, even if she is not acting out. But the child knows that what she is feeling is "bad"; she then perceives her Self as being bad.

In all of these instances, the result is that we leave childhood burdened by misperceptions of our Selves and our world. Interestingly, this kind of thinking is endemic in certain cultures, such as those that practice animistic religions—like the one from which the Garden myth arose thousands of years ago. They associated the constant struggle of hard daily life with the guilt and shame they felt within. Since this guilt and shame came out of their early struggle to achieve identity and autonomy, they put the two together and came up with a cause and effect: I feel guilt and shame; I must have done something wrong. These feelings came out of my struggle for identity and autonomy; therefore I am being punished for pursuing those goals.

In other words, all the hardships of life, including death, are explained as being punishment for being Self-aware and autonomous. How then do we reconcile this apparent and glaring inconsistency in the Creation myth? The next chapter will explore the reconciliation.

∞3∞

The Reconciliation

HOW DO WE RESPOND?

There are two ways in which we can respond to the Garden myth. We can accept it literally: we are indeed profoundly guilty for having disobeyed the God-Parent, for striving for Self-knowledge and autonomy. We are "something-wrong-with-us" human beings because we did so, and the difficulties we face in our lives are a punishment for this terrible transgression.

Or, we can look at the myth as an attempt to explain the condition of life by people with limited psychological-religious equipment: magical, egocentric thinking. This myth, like any other fairy tale, is a way of facing the reality of the world and the conflicts of our psychological needs.

Although the Garden story is religious in form, it is more like a fairy tale than an abstract theological treatise. Like most fairy tales, it tries to convey, in symbolic language, the profound and complex conflicts we all experience in the course of coming to maturity. The story of the Garden of Eden can be understood, then, as a religious fairy tale that wrestles with deep, universal, human conflicts.

I do not believe I am trivializing the Garden story by calling it a myth or comparing it to a fairy tale. Myths and fairy tales have great richness, and serve an important function in our lives. They help us to sort out the contents of our lives so that we are not continually traumatized by the conflicts we experience as part of our maturation process. Using fairy tales, we attempt to walk through the development crises we experience, and prepare our Selves for adult ways of thinking.

As children, we are particularly vulnerable to the conditions of survival, and on some level, we are aware of that vulnerability. We often compensate for that sense of vulnerability by viewing our parents as all-powerful, all-knowing, and always present. That way, we can feel safe and secure in our Selves.

There comes a point, however, in a child's development when her identity no longer needs to be enclosed in the identity of the parent. At that time—if everything has gone right during the developmental period—the child will be able to admit directly and up front that her parents are like everyone in the world; namely, they have their good points and their bad points.

The fairy tale is the intermediate step through which the child will finally be able to recognize that her parents are people like all others. Until that time, the child requires an untainted image of an all-perfect, all-loving parent. The fairy tale splits the "good" and "bad" parts of the parent into two distinct beings. For example, the "good" mother dies in Hansel and Gretel and the "bad" mother appears as the witch. The fairy tale helps the child begin to admit that his parents have faults, and is the intermediate step in this process.

THE AUTHORS OF THE STORY

The Garden myth, like the fairy tale, is an intermediate step in accepting our Selves as complex human beings. Before we delve deeper into the meaning of the story, however, we must first consider the authors of the Garden story. Who were they? No one knows for sure, but it is certain that whoever they were, they understood well the difficulties of living through normal human events. They also understood (even if they could not name) the vague but pervasive shame and guilt that seemed to emerge around issues of identity and autonomy.

Their fundamental experiences were the same then as ours are now. For example, most of us have experienced mixed feelings about leaving home in late adolescence or early adulthood. Most of us find that time emotionally tumultuous, and experience varying degrees of guilt and shame upon "abandoning" our parents.

The authors of the Garden story, and the people to whom it was addressed, had similar kinds of psychological conflicts. They were aware of these conflicts, and vaguely aware of their connection to the issues of identity and autonomy, but they didn't know precisely where they came from. The Garden story is their attempt to explain these conflicts.

In a way, they were trying to rationalize why "bad things happen to good people." They took their own feelings of shame and guilt associated with their quest for autonomy and identity, and used the characters of Adam and Eve to explain their existence. For the authors, what happened to Adam and Eve—existing first in the Garden, sheltered and protected, and then being cast out—explains their own feelings of guilt and shame. From the authors' viewpoint, Adam and Eve *must* have done something wrong.

Adam and Eve, the primeval children, the prototypes for all human children, disobeyed their "parent" when they empowered themselves to eat the forbidden fruit, thereby gaining Self-knowledge and autonomy. The struggle towards these psychological goals was experienced as "wrong" by them, and understood as being forbidden by their all-powerful, all-knowing, ever-present parent.

All-powerful, all-knowing, ever-present. . . . But these are God's attributes as well. To the child, parents bear these same qualities. Is it possible that the creators of the Garden myth transferred their feelings in response to and perceptions about their god-like earthly parents onto the heavenly parent?

WHOSE STORY IS IT?

There is a term in the field of psychotherapy that describes one of the ways in which humans relate to one another. The term is transference. An example of this would be: I meet a man at a party, and instantly dislike him. He's done nothing, said nothing, to justify my response to him. Yet I feel uneasy around him. Later, baffled by my intense response to him, I realize that this man reminded me of my brother (father, uncle, next door neighbor), who treated me badly as a child. At the party, I *transferred* my feelings and perceptions about my brother from my personal ancient history onto this perfect stranger.

I propose that the creators of the Garden myth transferred their feelings toward themselves in relationship with their god-like parents onto God-the-Heavenly-Parent. Thus, when we read the Garden story, we make the mistake of thinking (just as the creators of the story did) that God is telling the story, when it is really being told from Adam and Eve's human understanding.

GOD'S POINT OF VIEW

What if we change the point of view of the story from Adam and Eve's to God's? In order to do that, we must consider the story not just as the story itself, but in the context of the entire mythology. When we do that, we come up with a very different conclusion.

When we examine the history of salvation, namely God's attempt to appoint the people of Israel as his chosen ones, we constantly stumble over their inability to lay claim to that call. Instead, they continually revert to the worship of false gods, who demand sacrifices from them for the "wrong-doing" of their very existence. Their sense of worthlessness, guilt and shame does not allow them to place their trust in the true God, who has their best interests at heart.

No matter what prophet God sent to reaffirm His love for them, the people of Israel met the prophet with obstinacy, disbelief and hostility. Even if they had a change of heart, it was fairly short-lived. Soon they returned to their idol worship and the offering of the sacrifices. Because of the toxicity of their feelings of guilt and shame, they could not believe God could love them.

This pattern is repeated over and over and God's attempts to communicate His love for the people of Israel are constantly frustrated. Each time the pattern is repeated, God, in frustration, tries to intercede into their disbelief by arresting their attention with events like the rescue of His people from Egypt and their subsequent worship of the Golden Calf, or the foretelling of the fall of Jerusalem by Jeremiah in response to their worship of false gods.

Jesus, like the other prophets of Judaism, had a mission to challenge the Chosen People's cultural sense of worthlessness, guilt and shame before their loving God. But unlike the other prophets, Jesus was not just another human being. He was the manifestation of God on Earth. He had come to restructure the understanding and meaning of the Garden myth, to challenge our belief that there is something intrinsically wrong with who we are.

Jesus' job was to complete the mythological cycle—to tell the Creation story from God's perspective, and to set the stage for the necessity of the redemptive process. In this new view of the story, it is not God who has to forgive us and restore us unto Him, but we who have to forgive our Selves. We have imagined our Selves condemned by God, and we have been waiting for His forgiveness for something we have never done. We have it within our Selves to correct this misperception. It requires that we forgive our misunderstanding, and thereby forgive our Selves.

Jesus' purpose as Messiah was to confront and discount this perception we have about our Selves as worthless, and to release us from the bondage of the inner power that keeps us in a negative state of mind.

When we read the Garden story and realize that it is being told from Adam and Eve's perspective, does this deny the possibility that this story, or the whole Bible, was divinely inspired? No, it does not. It is my view that God was helping the "writers" of the Bible articulate human reality from the human perspective.

Furthermore, viewing the myth from the psychological perspective in no way invalidates the story or the religious content of it. To the contrary, it resolves the apparent and profound inconsistency between chapters one and three of Genesis. If that inconsistency could not be resolved, it would turn God into a trickster and a liar and someone who reneged on His promises.

Once we understand what our misperception of our relationship with God has been, we can resolve the conflict we have in relationship to our Selves, to other people and to Him. The Garden myth is an essential part of our history with God. In order for us to understand who we are in relation to Him, we must understand how we might have distorted God in our own eyes.

With this new and different understanding of the meaning of the Garden story and the total Judeo-Christian mythological cycle, we can now define original sin from a new perspective. Original sin has traditionally been defined as being a blemish on our soul, a state of shame and guilt because we committed some terrible, but undefined, act against God. The new definition of original sin is that the blemish on our soul is the misperception we have about our Selves; the failure to believe that we are created in the image and likeness of God.

ON TO MATURITY

Each child, like Adam and Eve, engages in a struggle for control, autonomy and Self-awareness. However, when we gain these things, we lose the privileges of paradise: perpetual care, comfort, and constant communion and intimacy with the parent (God). And since we have empowered our Selves to express our autonomy and identity, we believe it is that Self-empowerment that alienates us from paradise: we think we have done something wrong, that there is something wrong with us, and that we have sinned.

Just as each child perceives that he has brought upon his Self the alienation and wrath of his earthly parent(s), we as adults—including the adults who formulated the Garden story—transfer and project that conflict onto God-the-Heavenly-Parent. With this as the context for the Garden story, the creators perceived that their striving toward identity and autonomy brought upon them the wrath of God.

But to keep our understanding of God at the level proposed by the Garden of Eden story would be like keeping our understanding of our human parents at the level of fairy tales. If we are to achieve true adult maturity, so too must our understanding of God shift from the infant child perspective to something more adult. The following chapters will explore what that different perspective might be.

∽∾4∽∾

The Effects of Original Sin

JUDEO-CHRISTIAN MYTHOLOGY AND THE
STRUGGLE TO GET OUT OF THE GARDEN

How do we come to a more mature understanding of God? Christian mythology, from its perspective, brings the Judaic mythology full circle, and tells us that Jesus, as Messiah, Redeemer and God-Incarnate, came to Earth and entered into our reality to right the misunderstanding we have about our Selves and our relationship with God.

In this mythology, God, through the person of His Son Jesus, leads the way in the struggle to get beyond our internal, undefined, amorphous shame and guilt about our identity and autonomy. In fact, he enters our struggle so willingly and thoroughly that he actually lives it out, and dies at the hands of the powers of darkness that try to overtake us. But he also shows us that we can have a new life, and be victorious in that struggle.

Jesus' mission, in its simplest terms, was to reject the notion that we must live forever ashamed and guilty, to teach us to love our Selves, and to teach us to reclaim the love that was implanted within us in the creation event of chapter one of Genesis.

This is summarized in an interaction between Jesus and a lawyer. The lawyer asks Jesus, "Teacher, what is the greatest commandment?" Jesus answers that there are two great commandments: the first is to love the Lord God with all one's heart, mind and soul, and the second is to love one's neighbor as one's Self. Everything else flows from these two principles (Matt. 22:35–40).

By saying "you shall love your neighbor *as* yourself," Jesus sets up the love of Self as the central precept, with all other love flowing out of the love of Self.

A great many people, however, don't hear this message. They misinterpret what "love your neighbor" really means; they focus on that phrase, and fail to hear that the foundation of any love comes from the love of Self.

Why is there so much denial of the central principle of the greatest commandment of the law? Why are such enormous amounts of energy and mental gymnastics spent in rejecting this central precept of Jesus' teaching?

OUR OWN DEEP PLACE

Unfortunately for all of us, the human developmental process is flawed, and does not allow us to be free in Self-love and Self-knowledge. It is ironic that as we grow up, the very process by which we attain Self-identity and autonomy is the one that undermines us.

In some deep, dark place inside each of us, there is a part of the Self that believes it is devoid of any intrinsic worth. That part of the Self stands ashamed and guilty before all others, human and divine. Although this inner belief is stronger in some than in others, we all carry this internal burden around with us to some degree.

Because we believe that part of the Self is devoid of intrinsic worth, we are unable to love our whole Self fully. In my estimation, this is the source of the radical violence we do to our Selves and to each other, personally and collectively. There is a powerful void that we experience in the core of our consciousness. In that deep, private space, we experience our Selves as worthless; in that primal sense of worthlessness we consider our Selves profoundly unlovable.

This is the place of toxic shame and guilt that corrupts our souls. It is a grave secret that we have in us, a secret that many of us keep even from our Selves. But whether we admit the secret to our Selves or not, it rules us with an iron grip.

It is this secret that contradicts that which we know is right and motivates us to do that which we know is wrong. It is this secret that is the power of sin that Paul refers to in Rom. 7:15 when he says that this power makes him do not what he wants, but the very thing that he hates.

It is this secret, this inner falsehood, that alienates us from our Selves, each other and ultimately God. It is the lie to which we all cling; the lie that makes us hard of hearing, that makes us fight against God's message of light. It is the lie that Jesus came to dissolve.

Why is this failure to love our Selves so central to our dysfunction and why does Jesus proclaim so adamantly that love of Self is the reference point to love of others?

THE DYNAMICS OF SELF-HATRED

Each one of us is a unique manifestation of the Being of God. Each one of us is a particular facet on the jewel of the face of God, and reflects in our own, personal, unique way the Being of God. No one reflects the Being of God precisely in the same way I do, and no one reflects the Being of God in the totally unique way you do.

If I do not love my Self, I cannot accept or respect who I am as that special reflection of the Being of God. I relinquish my identity; I am unable to claim who I am. When I am unable to claim who I am, I am not there with and for my Self. I am not present to my Self. I do not know my Self. There is no sense of solidity or substance about the Self. I experience my Self as a void, a hole.

If I do not know my Self, and I do not love my Self, how can I possibly love another? I cannot. I cannot be present to anyone else, for I cannot be present within my Self. I become a void to my Self and to everyone else.

This scenario of Self-hatred is confirmed over and over again in my work as a pastoral psychotherapist. In session after session, this Self-hatred is clearly visible when a person is complimented, praised, or given a positive affirmation. It is amazing to me, even after all these years of practice, how often people are unable to hear or accept affirmations. It is even more amazing to me how often a positive affirmation can be perceived as a negative criticism or even a personal attack.

I remember one group session in particular in which this phenomenon was clearly demonstrated. A young man had been working through a number of very tough issues that had been brought up by other members of the group. After several months of laboring with these issues, the young man realized that he felt very grateful toward those others in the group who had helped him work through this difficult material. There were three people in the group he particularly wanted to thank. He thanked the first two, and then came to the third. He thanked her for her faithfulness, explaining why he was grateful.

As she was receiving this positive affirmation, this woman's face began to screw up into a mask of agony and pain. I asked her what was happening. She let out an incredible wail of pain, and said she heard an inner voice saying to her, "How could you put him through all of this pain? Shame on you!"

Because of all that inner noise, she was totally unable to hear the young man thanking her and affirming her for what she had done for him. She, like so many others of us, was caught in the belief system of toxic guilt, shame and worthlessness. She could neither affirm positive experiences of her Self, nor accept positive affirmation from others. The result was that she was caught in a Self-confirming downward spiral of Self-hatred and loathing that progressively fortified the internal experience of nothingness.

THE DYNAMICS OF SELF-LOVE

Total acceptance of the goodness of the Self generates Self-knowledge and Self-love. Self-knowledge and Self-love, in turn, generate an inner experience of substantiality (as opposed to emptiness and void) that communicates a sense of Self-worth. When *this* is the inner system we adhere to, we truly experience, and are able to confirm, the goodness of the Self.

When I am able to have true, *full* and unified love of Self, I come to know my Self. I *know* what it is to exist in that IAM place. With the fundamental experience of my own IAM-ness as my reference point, I can relate to others and understand the experience that is at the core of *their* being. The other person becomes more than a mere being to whom I can relate intellectually. Knowing my Self at the very core of I AM WHO I AM, I know the other person possesses that same awareness of her own IAM-ness within her Self.

The IAM experience is like the progressive opening of a flower. The original gift of IAM-ness is progressively revealed through living our lives in openness to our Selves and to each other. It is in this core experience of the IAM that we can have the most intimate knowledge of anyone—of our Selves, of another human, of God.

We can only assume that others experience their Selves as we experience our Selves. But, in the life beyond this one we will no longer be bound by the constraints of time and space. If we have been open to the intimacy of our own being we will be able to experience the being of another with the same intimacy with which we experience our own. Jesus himself says, "In that day, you will know that I am in the Father and you in me and I in you" (John 15–16).

In other words, when time and space no longer govern the conditions of our consciousness, we will know each other with the fullness that we know our Selves. In order to do that, however, Self-love and Self-knowledge have to be our reference points.

THE POWER OF OTHERS

Most of us do not use our Selves as reference points. Since we believe our Selves to be devoid of any intrinsic worth, we are convinced that we must look to others to alleviate our inner emptiness, shame and guilt. We think that gaining the approval and acceptance of others will affirm our inner value, worth and substance, and will fill up the abysmal void that lurks deep in the soul.

The problem is that it is never enough for any one person to say, "You're OK the way you are." Within this system, it is required that the whole world—everybody, without exception—regard us well.

Imagine a situation where I have just given a speech in front of hundreds of people. When I finish, I am greeted by thunderous applause. Backstage, I am mobbed by well-wishers. Everyone says I was wonderful—except for one woman, someone I don't even know. She says, "You were fine, but you mispronounced 'harassment.'" What do I think about for the rest of the night (if not the rest of my life)? How wonderful my speech was? No, I think about, and berate myself for, the fact that I mispronounced a word.

There could be one hundred people gathered around, telling us how wonderful we are. All it takes is one person who says, thinks (or we think is thinking), "You are not OK the way you are," and that statement, real or imagined, wipes away any positive Self-image we may have gained up to that point—and we are devastated. Every fiber of our being becomes organized around avoiding that single sentence in the hope that *every* person on the face of the Earth will say, "I like you, and you are OK the way you are."

This is the inner logic that drives many of us to live our lives always concerned about what others might think about us. It affects many of the choices we make and the activities we pursue. We unconsciously believe that others determine the value and worth of our being. We do not believe or experience our value and worth to be intrinsic to our Selves. We are compelled to become whatever *we think* others want us to be.

We are afraid to reveal our true, "worthless" inner Selves. We become afraid to make any statements of our own; to state with any clarity what we would like out of life, or even of the moment, becomes an event of massive anxiety. Demonstrating a feeling or perception, especially one that we have been taught to regard as "negative" like anger, frustration or disappointment, is too risky. To do so is to place our Selves in danger of spiritual death at the hands of "the other," whose murder weapon is the removal of acceptance and approval.

THE RAGE OF ORIGINAL SIN

When we are enmeshed within this internal system, we believe that our life depends upon the approval of others. If we believe that someone is taking away that approval, we believe that person is destroying our life. In the course of my work, I have come to recognize this way of thinking in what I call the "right/wrong" syndrome. The thinking goes like this:

- You disagree with me about something.
- If you disagree with me about something, it means that you don't approve of me.
- Since you disapprove of me, I am worthless. You have deprived me of my being.
- Depriving me of my being is the worst thing you can do to me.
- Therefore, I'm enraged with you for disagreeing with me.
- To save my being, I must prove to you that I am right (and therefore you are wrong).

It is not the actual disagreement we are enraged about, it is what the disagreement means in our minds: "I am devalued because you don't like me. If you did like me, you wouldn't disagree with me."

When disagreement means disapproval, our whole identity comes into question. We fight the disagree-er with volcanic fury. In this system, someone has to be right and the other person has to be wrong.

If agreement can't be reached (and I am ruled by toxic guilt), I automatically assume that *I* am the one who is wrong; if I am wrong, I am absolutely no good. Therefore, I must use every fiber of my being to convert the other person to my viewpoint, or to demonstrate beyond a shadow of a doubt that the other person is wrong.

What if the other person refuses to admit that he is wrong? The argument can never be concluded because, if I am bound in shame, I will "die" inside unless I obtain agreement or concession. To protect my Self from that "death of the soul," I will aim all my rage at the disagree-er in a frantic attempt to save my life.

Of course all of this intensifies if both people who are engaged in the argument operate out of the inner space of the toxic shame and guilt of original sin. The sad reality is that rage only makes the problem worse, for rarely is there any resolution to an argument whose energy is fueled by this system.

THE DISAPPEARING ACT

This system generates a tremendous amount of anxiety in us as we constantly look over our shoulders, worrying about who will or will not approve of our being. Instead of being our Selves, our goal is to become someone else, someone who is determined and defined by everyone else's concept of who we *should* be.

If this becomes our primary operating principle, our major endeavor in life is to hide the true Self. We define our Selves through what we believe are everyone else's concepts of who we are. We are desperate to please others, and we disappear within our Selves.

Not only do we disappear within our Selves, but the very people for whom we are doing the disappearing act vanish as well. On the surface, we appear to be concerned about others, always "tuned into" what they need or want. We bend over backwards to do something nice for them. When we are caught up within this belief system, however, the identity of the other person actually has little significance for us. The fundamental reason we are being nice is because we think it will purchase the sense of worth and value we attach to that person's approval.

In reality, though, we have little concept of the other person's needs. We are so busy figuring out what others want of us, and so much internal noise and confusion is generated in the figuring of it, we are unable to hear when someone *does* tell us what he actually needs or wants. We cannot be responsive to what the person *really* wants and needs, because we are so busy creating an internal mirage of the other person.

The end result of this internal system is a cruel irony. As we desperately attempt to avoid disappearance, we *do* disappear. We are left isolated because we are so lost within our inner construction that we lose touch with the real person "out there." We experience our Selves as empty voids because we have evacuated our inner substance in deference to the other.

And, because we are so lost in the inner world we have constructed, the possibility of someone else actually touching us and affirming our substantiality is either severely damaged or lost entirely to us as well. The result is that the experience of Self is lost to us in both the inner and interpersonal worlds. Instead of living out Jesus' commandment to love our neighbor, in this system we do not love our neighbor, we do not love our Selves—we end up loving no one.

Sadly, many people think that to be "Christian" means to become Self-less, to disappear in deference to the needs, wants, desires, feelings, perceptions and thoughts of others at the expense of our own. When we fall victim to this internal system, our Christianity becomes an inversion of the pinnacle of the Law as it was articulated by Jesus.

∞5∞

I Am Who I Am Re-Affirmed

REHEARING THE CHRISTIAN MYTH

Jesus defines the love of Self as the central point of reference by which we love and respond to the world around us. In so doing, he presents a system of spirituality and religion that contradicts the one presented in the Garden myth.

Rather than being guilty and ashamed of who we are and experiencing our Selves as empty shells, we are instructed to love and affirm our Selves. We are to feel the pulse of life within us so that we can love and respect that in others. When Jesus reveals this as God's central law, he brings us back to the goodness of chapter one of Genesis.

It is only when we love and respect our Selves, not in the abstract, but in the real circumstances of our lives, that we can we hear and respond to the true IAM-ness of our neighbors. When we examine Jesus' teachings and how he responded to people in general, we find that he affirms the love of the Self and its central place in his spiritual teachings through a multitude of stories, sayings and actions.

THE GOODNESS OF CREATED CONSCIOUSNESS

We all leave our personal Garden of Eden (our infancy) believing that, in the name of identity and autonomy, we have committed some terrible sin against our Creator. And, because of this terrible sin, we believe we bear the curse of the pain of living. We worry about everything—about how we will get the necessities (and the luxuries) of life, and about how we will survive.

Jesus counters our belief in that sin and its curse in the wonderful discourse of the birds and the lilies. He describes how the birds eat freely, and how the lilies are clothed in a natural loveliness even Solomon, in all his glory, could not rival (Matt. 6:25–32). He points out that the birds have plenty of food and the lilies have their beauty without worrying about it, so why should we worry about having what we need? He adds that the Heavenly Parent knows we need material things, but that we have a higher calling. If we seek instead the Lord's righteousness, material things will be given to us as well.

But what does the "Lord's righteousness" mean? According to Webster's dictionary, to be righteous means to act according to divine or moral law, free from guilt or sin. This is the Law that Jesus came to reveal: to love God above all; to love my Self as a reflection of God's being within me; and to respond to my neighbor with the same love I have for my Self.

Jesus is talking about more than just food, clothing and shelter in the parable of the birds and the lilies; he is also addressing what these things *mean* to us. We worry about how we appear to others if we are not dressed, housed or fed in a particular way (or educated at a particular school, associated with the right people, think the right way, behave according to other peoples' norms, raise "perfect" children, and so on). We worry that others will think less of us if we do not measure up to the criteria we *think* they hold for us. We believe that if we do not measure up, our sense of value about our Selves will be destroyed. This anxiety about appearances overtakes our souls. As a result, we lose sight of the fact that we have life and the divine consciousness throbbing within us.

Referring to the birds and the lilies, Jesus asks the question, "But are you not of more value than they?" In that question, he seems to be implying, "After all, aren't you made in the image and likeness of that same God who takes care of the birds of the air and the lilies of the field? The birds do not have to sow or reap, yet they are taken care of. The lilies do not toil or spin, yet they are taken care of. Therefore, why worry that you will not be taken care of?" It as though he chides us for not knowing that God truly loves us and regards us well in the first place. Do we not know that we will be provided for *because* God loves us?

It would seem then that it was Jesus' commission to relay to us that we have been laboring under a misconception about our Selves and our relationship with God.

Jesus is challenging the belief that we have to "do" something, or become other than who we are if we are to have any meaning and value. Instead, he is encouraging us *to* be who we are, in the image and likeness of God, existing in the goodness in which we were created. When we lose sight of that, we dishonor the YHWH consciousness within us.

Not only does Jesus absolve us from the sin we think we committed in the Garden of Infancy when we pursued our identity and autonomy, he also releases us from the curse we think was uttered against us when we were supposedly expelled. We think that the realities of daily life, work, toil, pain, sickness, and death are punishments for being bad people. He says instead that these are the realities of life, and they have nothing to do with our goodness and worth. This suggests that there was no curse to begin with, for God has always loved us; we were never condemned by our Creator for being who we are.

Jesus reveals to us that being created in the image and likeness of God, and being good and blessed by God, is our birthright and our fundamental reality. Our inability to accept this concept interrupts the flow between our Selves and God, and causes us to miss the mark of what God has in mind for us.

According to the *Dictionary of the Bible*, edited by John L. McKenzie, S.J., missing the mark of what God has in mind for us is the ancient definition and understanding of sin. We are in sin, missing the mark, when we do not regard our Selves well. We tend to underestimate who we are. Most of us commit sins of pride (overestimating our Selves) not because we think too much of our Selves, but because we think too little of our Selves. We over*exaggerate* our importance in an attempt to compensate for the unconscious disregard we have for our Selves.

THE WORTH OF THE IAM: JESUS' EXAMPLE

Jesus does not only preach Self-love and respect and the worthiness of the individual, he practices it as well. There is the story of a dinner party at which a woman comes up to Jesus with an alabaster flask of very expensive ointment. She pours the ointment on his head as he sits at the table.

Some at the party are indignant and question what they consider to be a wasteful act. They argue that the ointment might be sold for a large sum and given to the poor. But Jesus contradicts them, saying that the woman has done a beautiful thing by honoring him in this way. He adds that the poor will always be with them, but he himself will not always be there (Matt. 26:6–13).

By saying this, Jesus indicates that we cannot, or should not *always* consider the needs of others before our Selves. He demonstrates the positive regard we are to have for our Selves that, at times, takes precedence over responding to the needs of others. He models for us the original commandment he has given, in which the love of Self precedes the love of the other.

In another instance, when Jesus hears that John the Baptist has been beheaded (Matt. 14:13–22), he goes off to pray, presumably to mourn

John's death. But a crowd of people, also hearing of John the Baptist's death, follow Jesus and disrupt his solitude.

When Jesus finds the crowd waiting for him, he compassionately ministers to them, cures the disabled of their afflictions, and teaches them the consoling word of God. When the day begins to draw to a close, there is a shortage of food. The crowd of five thousand has only five loaves of bread and two fishes to eat. Jesus then performs the miracle of the multiplication of the loaves and fishes, and everyone is satisfied. Finally, though, Jesus decides that enough is enough. He sends his disciples away in a boat to distract the crowd. He, in turn, goes off in a third direction to replenish his Self in prayer.

Here Jesus demonstrates the tension that exists in balancing the needs of the Self against the needs of others. Jesus momentarily puts aside his own need for solitude and prayer to respond to the urgency of the people who followed him. However, he ultimately returns to his own need to restore his IAM through prayer.

As in the episode of the precious ointment, he demonstrates that there is a limit to giving to the other when the health of the soul, the IAM, is at stake. He sets up a model for all of us to follow: we are to respond to the needs of others, sometimes with a degree of sacrifice, but the sacrifice must end when it endangers the health of the soul, the integrity, substantiality, uniqueness or autonomy of the Self.

THE IAM QUALITIES

Through these and other incidents, Jesus affirms the sanctity of each individual, human IAM, the respect we are to have for our Selves, and the respect we are to have for others.

But he also affirms the various qualities that are intrinsic to the IAM state of being:

1. the fact of our IAM-ness;
2. the uniqueness of the IAM;
3. the separateness or autonomy of the IAM;
4. the integrity of the IAM;
5. the inner empowerment of the IAM;
6. the timelessness of the IAM;
7. the sense of inner substance as a person in the experience of these other qualities.

THE AFFIRMATION OF IAM-NESS

On that Easter morning years ago, as I looked out on the scene that lay before me and first became aware of my unique identity within my IAM-ness, I experienced what I now call "stimulation states." As I sit here, now, attempting to articulate these concepts to my Self and to you, I am in stimulation states. I feel my fingers press against the keyboard, and my back up against the chair in which I sit. Whenever I engage another person in conversation, the process by which we hear and exchange pointsof view results in stimulation states. My Self-awareness comes to life through these stimulation states, and I discover, experience and appreciate the fullness of my own IAM-ness.

Various philosophers have articulated this concept over the centuries: in medieval times it was known as *"Sentio ergo sum,"* i.e., "I feel, therefore, I am." Later, Descartes said *"Cogito ergo sum,"* i.e., "I think, therefore, I am." My thoughts and feelings are not my Self-awareness, but they are the vehicle through which I experience it. Through them, my IAM-ness is revealed to me.

Uniqueness

When I accept and operate out of the internal truth that I AM WHO I AM, the only person who reflects the consciousness of God in my one of a kind way, then I experience my uniqueness.

However, when I accept and operate out of the belief that I have to conform to what I think others want me to be, I become other-than-who-I-am. I deny my specialness as the IAM who has been created to reflect God in my unique way.

Jesus reminds us to honor our uniqueness with wonderful light imagery (Matt. 5:14–16). He calls each one of us the light of the world; we are called into being to shine for all to see. What sense would it make to light a lamp and then cover it? None.

So why, he challenges us, would God create us and then ask us to hide who we are? That doesn't make sense either. Rather, he tells us, we are to shine before all so that all may see the goodness that is within, thereby giving glory to the Creator.

We are not to hide who we are, nor are we to hide the uniqueness of our being. We are to proclaim our unique IAM-ness to the whole world. To do otherwise is to reject the love of God as it is reflected in the gift of our special consciousness.

Autonomy

Autonomy, in terms of IAM-ness, depends on three things:

1. I realize my substantiality, that this is me in here;
2. I realize that I am separate from you;
3. I realize that my existence, especially my spiritual existence, does not depend on you.

When Eve and Adam decided to eat of the fruit of the tree, they decided to act independently of God. In so doing, the claimed their autonomy. Because they became autonomous, they thought they had committed a terrible sin and were worthless as a result. Jesus displays a different attitude toward autonomy both in the way in which he lived out his life and in what he taught.

When he was twelve years old, Jesus, Joseph and Mary went with many other people to the city of Jerusalem to celebrate Passover. After the celebration, Joseph and Mary were a day's journey beyond the city when they realized that Jesus was not with the rest of the relatives. Worried, probably even panicked, they rushed back to Jerusalem and searched for him for three days. They finally found him in the temple, listening to the learned men and offering them very profound questions and responses. His parents, understandably upset, asked him why he had caused them such anxiety. He responded that they should have known that he would be in his Father's house (Luke 2:41–52).

His response to his parents is typical of a twelve-year-old. Many of us would have reacted to this "smart aleck" response by telling him in no uncertain terms that he shouldn't talk to his parents that way and that he had better not do such a stupid thing ever again.

Instead Joseph and Mary said little to him. They did not shame him for his *act of autonomy* from them. They apparently realized that he was becoming an adult, a person who had an identity separate from theirs—even though his act of autonomy had caused them pain and anxiety. The message to us from this story is that autonomy from our parents is normal, appropriate and necessary—even if it results in pain and anxiety for them.

Another instance of an act of autonomy on Jesus' part occurred when he was about twenty-nine or thirty, at a wedding in Cana (John 2:1–11). At one point, Mary overhears that the wine has run out. She approaches Jesus and informs him that there is no more wine, implying that he could do something about it if he wished. Jesus seemingly rebukes her when he says, "Woman, why do you trouble me? My time has not yet come." Yet he does, in fact, reveal his Self by changing water into wine, thereby formally beginning his ministry.

This story has often been interpreted as an example of Jesus bending to the will of his mother. If that were the case, however, why does Jesus rebuke his mother? It could be that the rebuke is a response to her attempt to control how and when he would manifest his Self. It seems, as he reflects on the event, that *he* decides *for himself* that it is time for him to manifest his Self. By changing the water into wine at this event, *he* decides to reveal his Self and his mission in the world.

Through this story, Jesus once again affirms the need to be separate from our parents. Further, when a parent (or parental figure) inappropriately intrudes upon the autonomy of an adult child, that child has the right and responsibility to rebuke the parent for doing so. So Jesus is instructing us through his own life experience that autonomy is not only *not sinful*, but a necessary part of the human condition.

Integrity

One of the essential qualities of the IAM is that of integrity: being whole and undivided within one's Self. This means we must have an awareness of our corporeal beings (our bodies, alive in the material world), and our spiritual beings (our IAM-ness, alive in our inner world). In order for the continual process of Self-awareness to take place, there must be unity between the reality of existence in this time and place, and the spiritual dimension of the IAM. We must be in touch with our inner Selves and with the outer world so that we can experience the stimulation states described above.

When we disown our thoughts, feelings and perceptions, our spectrum of stimulation states becomes severely impoverished. We chop the total Self into disparate parts. We exist in a fractured state in which some parts of our Selves are alienated and disowned by other parts. The Self is in a state of disintegration.

When there is dissociation by the Self from its thoughts, feelings and perceptions, the IAM itself is in danger of disintegration, because the vehicles (the stimulation states) through which the IAM reveals itself are severely curtailed or lost. The gift of Self-awareness that was granted us by God upon our creation becomes badly tarnished.

The most intense pain we can suffer is when we disown who we are by splitting off the parts of our Selves we think are unacceptable to others.

It is the pain of the disintegration of the Self and the IAM consciousness that lies in the center of the Self. However, this pain alerts us to that fact that we are destroying our most precious gift, the gift of our IAM-ness, our existence in the image and likeness of God.

We cause the disintegration of the Self when we deny our own perceptions of reality. If we think someone has violated us, for instance, we do not face that perception and work it out with the other person. We deny the perception altogether.

Consider the following scenario as an example: I loaned my friend Richard $100.00, which he said he would pay back in a month. The month has now passed, and he has not returned the money. Because my inner system tells me I am not allowed to express my thoughts and feelings to other people, I stop my Self from calling Richard and asking for an explanation.

Instead, I lose my Self in a world of make believe; I construct my own version of Richard's reality. I believe in and adhere to this version with leech-like tenacity, and I now think that Richard is a horrible person who never had any intention of paying me back. Furthermore, since my inner system tells me that I am a person of no worth, Richard's nonpayment confirms to me that I am not worthy of being paid back.

My misperception is that Richard is a horrible person who has seen into my soul—and my worthlessness. I hate him, secretly, of course. My conclusion is not only that I can never trust Richard again—but that I can't really trust anyone else again, either.

What I don't know is that Richard gave a check to a mutual friend to deliver to me, but the friend forgot all about it. Since my Inner Other forbids me to reveal my perceptions, as well as my "negative" feelings of anger and frustration, to Richard, I do not get the one piece of information (that Richard gave our friend the check) that would have completely changed my perceptions of and feelings toward Richard and, by extension, of my Self and the whole human race.

We've all been through similar situations. Part of us knows we're creating stories. The part of the Self that *does* perceive what is happening is pushed into a corner and ignored as though it doesn't exist, and we function as though we are chopped up into a multitude of parts, all at war with one another. Each of the stories we create has its own emotional content, and they all tend to bump into each other. Thus, we've created emotional conflict over a situation like this one that doesn't even really exist.

This phenomenon occurs because we have an inner agenda against confrontation. We deny our Selves the opportunity to confront the situation directly and get the information we need to proceed rationally. Instead, we isolate our Selves from the other person. We also become isolated from our Selves because we give up the chance of working through our own perceptions (true or false). We become frustrated and angry at our Selves because of the emotional conflicts we've created by constructing elaborate stories instead of facing reality. The Self-directed anger that his emotional conflict generates further undermines our already weakened sense of and love for the Self.

Jesus, however, presents a very different psychology and theology when he says: "The eye is the lamp of the body. If your eye is sound, your whole Self will be full of light; but if your eye is not sound, the whole Self will be full of darkness. If the light in you is darkness, how great is that darkness!" (Matt. 6:22–23).

Jesus challenges us to respect what we see with our eyes (and hear with our ears). If we don't, we disown our own reality and become full of darkness. We lose touch with our Selves and with others.

On the other hand, if we can remain true to our Self when we perceive there is something wrong between our Self and the other, we have a base from which we can work out the problem. We can go to the person, confront him with the perceived wrongdoing, and:

1. find out that our perception was incorrect, enabling us to "let go" of the problem;
2. make the other person aware of the problem, allowing him or her to apologize and correct the difficulty; or
3. discover that the person is insensitive and unwilling to respect our IAM-ness, in which case we face the fact that this may be an inappropriate relationship, and one we may need to dissolve.

In Matt. 18:15–17, Jesus tells the disciples that if your brother sins against you, you should go and tell him, in private, what he has done. If he listens to you, the better for both of you. But if he does not listen, then he is to be to you as the publican or the tax collector—he is to be excluded from your life. In other words, we are to protect our sacred IAM-ness from abuse by those who cannot respect our being.

To be true to one's Self in this way brings inner strength and integrity—the full inner light of being in the IAM. To do the opposite is to deny the IAM and to dwell in profound darkness, for it is not only our perceptions that we deny; we deny our needs as well, capitulating them deferentially to the needs of others. There is a story about Jesus visiting his friends Lazarus, Martha and Mary at their home in Bethany (Luke

10:38–42). After he arrives, the men gather about him and the conversation begins. Mary comes in, sits down and becomes absorbed in the discourse. Meanwhile, Martha is in the kitchen, serving many dishes and playing the perfect hostess. Finally her exasperation spills over. She complains to Jesus that Mary has left her to take care of everything by herself, and she wants Jesus to tell Mary to come help her.

Jesus gently but pointedly tells Martha that she really didn't need to be doing so much. One dish would have served them as well as many, and he could not fault Mary for choosing to remain and listen to his teachings.

Many of us are just like Martha, always busy doing for someone else, never taking the time to do for our Selves. When we do this over a long period of time (maybe even a whole lifetime), we begin to fall apart, to disintegrate within the depths of our being.

When that happens, we float in a sea of chronic but vague resentment. We experience the disintegration of the Self and the evaporation of the IAM consciousness. We blame other people. Our resentment oozes out, like it did for Martha, when we think that we are being exploited by others. The fault is, in fact, our own failure to adequately define boundaries for our Selves. The failure to respond to our own needs becomes a life-long pattern that results in a profound inner sense of disintegration, and robs us of the ability to harness the energy of our life flow.

Jesus, however, does not buy into Martha's system. Instead, in a compassionate, understanding but firm way, he admonishes her for the inner demands she places upon her Self. He does not allow her to blame Mary *or himself*. He does not accept responsibility for Martha's inability and/or unwillingness to claim her own needs. In other words, to use a currently popular term, Jesus refuses to enter into a codependent relationship with Martha by supporting her dysfunctional inner system. He recognizes that her resentment is generated by her own need to "do for others," and not by Mary's lack of assistance. By addressing Martha the way he does, he gently, compassionately, but firmly tells all of us that he, and therefore God, will not support those who complain about others' exploitation when they themselves are unwilling to define their own boundaries.

Substantiality

Substantiality is a trait of the IAM-ness in which I experience myself solidly *within my Self*. A sense of substantiality is an outgrowth of the uniqueness and the integrity of the Self.

When we cave in to the needs and perceptions of others without reference to our own, our sense of personal IAM-ness darkens. Our uniqueness fades, and our wholeness as integrated persons crumbles into disparate parts that are often at battle with each another.

The IAM experience, as a result, begins to evaporate like a mist. Because of the fracturing and disassociation of the outer layers of the Self from the core of the Self, the IAM is so diffuse that we experience a deep sense of inner void.

Jesus tells us that we must treasure that which we are: "You are the salt of the earth; but if the salt has lost its savor, how shall its saltness be restored? It becomes worthless, not good for anything except to be thrown out and trodden under feet" (Matt. 5:13). Once the savor of the salt has disappeared, it has lost its "saltness," and lost its value. If we don't claim who we are, we lose our savor; we lose that which gives us meaning, substance.

We must claim our Selves in the day-to-day existence of our lives. If I see something, I have to claim that I saw it and take it from there. If I need something, I must do the same (that doesn't necessarily mean I'll get it; I still have to claim that I need it). To live out my moment-to-moment existence in any other way means that I disrespect my IAM-ness as it is manifested in this moment of time—which is the only moment I have to be in my IAM-ness.

This is confirmed in the parable of the wise and foolish persons, each of whom builds a house. The wise one builds her house on rock (the substantiality of her IAM-ness). That house survives wind and rain and flood, because it is built on solid foundation. On the other hand, the foolish person (who does not believe in the sanctity of her IAM-ness) builds her house upon sand. When the storms of life come, this house crashes to the ground because its foundation is weak and unstable (Matt. 7:24–27).

We are the foolish person when we build the house of our soul upon the shifting sands of the opinions of others. When we build our existence on the solid rock of our moment-to-moment IAM-ness, we know our Selves as solid, full of life and unshakable. We begin to experience a sense of worth and fullness about our Selves we have rarely experienced before. It is then that we finally become the children of God, centered in the unique IAM-ness of our being.

The Ever-Present

The person who sits here thinking these thoughts and typing them into the word processor is the same person, the same, unchanged consciousness who sat, as a child of four, on the back steps of his parents' home beginning to realize his own uniqueness and autonomy. This person, this I AM WHO I AM, whose one-of-a-kind uniqueness goes by the name of Jack, exists outside of the past and the future. In the core of his consciousness, he exists only in the ever-present now.

For that part of my being there is no past or future, there is only the unchangeable reality of consciousness that exists without any time reference. It is always *now*.

In my work, I have found that my clients' most persistent pain and distraction is caused by their attempts to control the future, their future, and the world's future. They constantly worry: "What *will* happen if I say this . . . ?" "What *will* happen if I do that . . . ?" What they're really thinking is, "If I say this, do that, live here, dress this way, or associate with those people, I won't be liked—and then I'll be nothing." It is this distraction that lifts us out of the present, the place of the IAM, and catapults us into the unreal place of the not-here-yet future.

When we live our lives as though the future is already here, we are not present to the now, and we are one step removed from our IAMness. If we live our lives based on some future event that we *think* is going to happen, the ever-present quality of the IAM evaporates.

This does not mean that we cannot plan ahead. There is a great difference between planning for the future and operating as though we already know what the future holds.

We can *plan* for a future event while staying rooted in the present. Consider this scenario: I realize that I like to write, that it gives me a great sense of satisfaction and fulfillment. I decide I'd like to improve my writing skills, and do some research as to how I might do that. I make plans to go back to school, or to attend a local workshop. My goal is to write a book someday. By doing the research, enrolling in courses, and practicing writing, I am living in the present, but planning for the future.

Many people, however, catapult themselves out of the present directly into an imagined future. In this scenario, I realize that I like to write, but I immediately begin to worry about what people might think of my writing goals. When I think about taking classes, I worry about what other people will think of my writing, and how they will judge me for writing so poorly. So I put off going to school, and stop writing altogether.

In the first example, I can plan for the future because I am aware of something about my present Self—in this case, that I like to write. As a result of that present experience, I can organize each successive present moment and move toward a goal, existing in the present moment throughout.

In the second example I predict (however falsely) what people *will* think about me. I move out of my own existence and try to enter into the other people's. I alter my present (by making a decision *not* to go back to school) based on a false assumption about the future, and operate as though the future is already here. Based on my "knowledge" of the future, I make my choices for today. I believe I know the future better than I know the present. When that happens, I violate the intrinsic ever-present quality of the IAM.

When Jesus tells the story of the birds of the air and the lilies of the field, he is addressing the issue of the ever-present quality of the IAM and the dangers of spending all our time being anxious and worried. He tells us that fretting over things neither adds to nor subtracts from the length of our lives. Therefore, we don't need to be anxious about tomorrow for tomorrow will happen without any help from us. Today is real; don't leap into the future by worrying about it. Stay in the ever-present now and enjoy the gifts of the day.

THE SINNER'S INTRINSIC WORTH

Jesus tells us, through these stories and parables, that we are intrinsically good and blessed. We learn that certain acts we think of as wrong are really right and natural. However, as we have all experienced, there are times when a person is "bad"—that is, when a person does something to violate her Self or others. When this happens, Jesus tell us that it is the act that is bad, and not the person. He draws a distinct line between the wrong act and the intrinsic value of the wrongdoer.

This is demonstrated in the story of Zacchaeus, a tax collector. As the story goes, Jesus is passing through a crowd of people in Jericho when he spots Zacchaeus. Jesus immediately invites himself to Zacchaeus' home. When Zacchaeus hears this, he is startled and then overjoyed at being chosen for this honor. Recognizing that he has been greedy and exploited the people, Zacchaeus repents of all the things he has done to abuse his office. He tells Jesus that he will give half his goods to the poor and that if he has defrauded anyone of anything, he will restore it fourfold. Jesus responds by saying, "Salvation has come to this house. The Son of Man has come to seek out and save the lost" (Luke 19:1–10).

Jesus does not condone Zacchaeus' material exploitation of others. However, Jesus makes it clear by inviting himself to Zacchaeus' home *before* he has repented of his sins, that he is loved by the virtue of his existence as a created I AM, a child of God. The worth and value of Zacchaeus' soul was never lost or destroyed because of his wrongdoing. What *was* harmed was the bond between Zacchaeus and God. What Jesus is emphatically saying is that even with the bond damaged between them, Zacchaeus' intrinsic worth as a person remains intact.

When we are in a chronic (and often times acute) state of toxic guilt and shame, we find it very difficult to separate our mistakes from our worth. We search for confirmation of the worthlessness of our souls, and we find it in myths like the Garden story, which tells us that God considers our souls to be decayed as well. But in the interchange with Zacchaeus, Jesus dispels this persistent notion we have about our Selves in no uncertain terms.

GOD'S PERSISTENT AFFIRMATION

There is a parable Jesus tells of a judge who was hard and overbearing and a woman who pestered him endlessly to make judgment against her adversary. Initially, the judge resisted her pleas. But she persisted, and he gave in for fear she would finally wear him out. Jesus makes the point that, if a hard man would finally hear the woman because of her persistence, would not the Lord God hear anyone who might cry out to be vindicated? But he adds, will anyone hear God's love for His children (Luke 18:1–8)?

God does not respond to us because we pester Him; He responds because of the intrinsic goodness that resides in each one of us. To deny that is to refuse the goodness of God's love itself. The question Jesus raises at the end of the story is, are we willing to hear that, or will we turn a deaf ear to the Lord's affirmation of our goodness?

At another point, he directs his followers to ask of the Heavenly Parent and assures them, in asking, they will receive what they seek. He then poses a question to them, "Which of you, if a child of yours asks you for bread or fish, will give that child a stone or a viper?" The answer, of course, is that none of them would do a thing like that. Then, he tells them that the Holy Parent, because of Her deep love for Her children whom She created out of love, will do all the more (Matt. 7:7–11). In spite of our own limits and faults, God loves and responds to us because we are Her children.

WE ARE NOT BAD BECAUSE OF PAIN AND TOIL

This principle is reaffirmed from a different perspective when Jesus challenges the religious leaders of his time to rethink their assumptions about a person's fundamental worth. In the Jewish theology of the time (and in the tradition of the Garden punishment) it was believed that physical handicaps or illness were the result of the individual's or family's sin. The sin was presumed to be there simply because the handicap existed.

One day, Jesus and his disciples pass a man blind since birth (John 9). As they go by him, his disciples question Jesus as to who committed the sin that made him blind, the man or his parents. Jesus' response to their question is that no one has committed any sin but rather this man is blind so that the power of God might be manifest through him. Jesus then spits into the dust, creates an ointment of clay, puts it on the man's eyes and tells him to wash in the nearby pool. When he does, he discovers he can see.

In a very direct way, Jesus counters the theology of the time in his verbal response and in the healing of the man. But, like us, the religious leaders refuse to believe that the theology of toxic shame and guilt has been abrogated. They will not believe that the theology of worthlessness has been repealed by the messenger of God. But, by denouncing the theory that blindness is a punishment for sin, and by restoring the man's sight, it has been. The shame, guilt and punishment of the apparent Garden sin has been dissolved.

THE GARDEN MYTH RECONCILED

Jesus came to us as God Incarnate, the Son of the Father-Protector and the Mother-Spirit-Nurturer, to set the record straight. He came to proclaim that the toxic guilt and shame we suffer is not born out of a wrongdoing acted out against God; rather it is a sad and burdensome misunderstanding that has built a wall between our Selves and God. In order for us to live harmoniously within our Selves, with each other and with God, we must give up the tightly held belief in an internal destitution that is born out of that false guilt and shame.

God created us in His image and likeness which gives us, at the very essence of our being, the substance and worth for which we all search so intently. To deny that inner substance and worth is to reject the most profound act of love possible—that God infused in us the essence of His being, to be I AM WHO I AM. When anyone or any power denies this, he or she blasphemes the name of God.

PART II

Jesus and Our Inner Demons

∞6∞

The Demonic Power: The Power of Toxic Guilt and Shame

OPPOSITION TO WORTHFULNESS

Why is it so difficult for humans to hear and accept messages of love and positive regard? Over the years, I've found that this resistance is one of the most difficult issues people have to confront—whether the positive messages come from me, from a group member, a spouse, a friend, a stranger—or even God. Our inner resistance to a positive message can, at times, be overwhelming.

God, through Jesus, beckons to us to let go of our resistance to His love for us, to be absolved of the guilt and shame we feel about who we are. Instead, He asks us to accept who we are, illuminated from within by the light of the conscious creative energy of the Holy One that lives within us.

We do not, however, easily let go of this resistance. In fact, the belief in our sense of "badness" about our Selves, and the resultant guilt and shame, grip us so completely that it required God's own Son to try and convince us differently. For his efforts, he himself met with massive resistance, persecution and ultimately murder for modeling and preaching this. What are the forces empowered within us that render us so blind and deaf to our own intrinsic goodness that we will murder the Son of God when he comes to counter these negative beliefs?

THE DEMONIC IN JESUS' LIFE

In the Christian mythology, there are numerous references to and stories about evil spirits, powers of darkness and Satan (Matt. 12:43–45; 8:16–17; 4:23–25; 8:28–34; Mark 5:1–20; 9:14–19; 1:13; 3:10–12; 7:24–30; Luke 8:26–39; 4:40–43; 6:17–19; 11:24–26).

For instance, more often than not, accounts of Jesus healing the crowds contain an exorcism of an individual or individuals who are possessed with evil spirits. When he meets the person's demons, he confronts them and casts them out, usually over the loud objections of the evil spirits. Further, Jesus warns his disciples that the most difficult cures involved demons and evil spirits, not healing the lame or the blind (Mark 9:29).

Just before Jesus was to begin his own ministry, he himself was tempted by the most powerful demon of all—Satan (Matt. 4:1–11). Jesus went out into the wilderness and fasted for forty days and forty nights. He was hungry. Satan came to him and said that if he was indeed the Son of God, he should be able to turn stones to loaves of bread. Jesus replied, "A person shall not live by bread alone, but from every word that proceeds from the mouth of God." Then the devil took him to the roof of the temple and dared him to throw himself down, for it was written that angels would "bear you up, lest you strike your foot against a stone." But Jesus replied that it was also written, "You shall not tempt the Lord your God." Lastly, Satan took Jesus to a high mountain, showed him all the kingdoms of the world, and promised they would be his if he would only fall down and worship him. But Jesus told him very clearly to be gone, for it was written, "You shall worship the Lord your God and him only shall you serve."

In this power struggle between Jesus and Satan, Jesus does not allow evil to rule him in any way. But through this encounter, Jesus demonstrates that this power struggle is an integral part of the human reality from which even he is not exempt. Rather, it is because he is also human that he must encounter that part of the human reality as well.

THE POWER OF DARKNESS

In John's Gospel there is no direct confrontation with Satan as it is depicted in the other three Gospels. Instead, Jesus frequently refers to the struggle between the powers of light and darkness, how they interact with us and how we respond to each of them. The writer refers to Jesus as the light that shines in the darkness. But, as John points out, even though Jesus is the light and his light is available to us, many choose not to accept him as such. And those who do not accept him as the light choose the darkness instead (1:9–11). In 3:19 he comments on how we humans love the dark rather than the light. Later, Jesus assures us that those who follow him will not walk in darkness, but will instead possess the light of life (8:12).

As the struggle between Jesus and the religious power elite is building to its climax, Jesus refers to himself as the light who will be with the disciples only a little longer. He encourages them to walk in that light while they still have the chance, warning them that the darkness may overtake them if they do not take advantage of the light while they have it (John 12:35). Then, he tells his disciples that who ever believes in him will not remain in darkness (John 12:46).

In his letters, John (1 John 1:5–9) speaks of Jesus as the light in whom no darkness resides. He goes on to describe our human struggle and contradiction:

- On the one hand, if we claim to be in union with God while in fact we live in darkness, we deceive our Selves.
- If we say, on the other hand, that we are without sin, that we are not influenced by the dark power that tempts us into sin, we deceive our Selves also.

What we must do is walk in the light of the Christ so that we may better see the deceptions of the dark power; and so that when it entraps us in its power, when we are tempted by it or even fall prey to it, we can pull our Selves out of its snare.

Later (1 John 2:8–11), John says that the darkness is fading away because of the light of the Christ. However, he quickly reminds us that if we do not follow God's commandment to love our fellow human beings, we will be blinded by the darkness once again.

PAUL AND THE POWER OF THE DARKNESS AND SIN

John is not the only one who refers to powers of darkness and light. In Romans 7, Paul speaks of a powerful "law of sin" within him that seduces him to override his best intentions. It is a power that is in direct contradiction to the Law of God that he so desperately wishes to follow.

In describing his own struggle with this power, he communicates that this is a struggle all human beings experience. He instructs us to discard the works of darkness and be fortified in the light instead (Rom. 13:12). Being so fortified, we will exist in the light which will then reveal what heretofore has been hidden in darkness (1 Cor. 4:5): the knowledge of the glory of God that is known through the face of the Christ (2 Cor. 4:6).

In Paul's letter to the Ephesians (5:5–14), he describes this struggle between the darkness and light in even greater relief. He tells us that we are the children of light and admonishes us to avoid those who worship idols because they walk in the darkness. He reminds us that we our Selves were once the children of that same darkness, and how easy it is for us to return to that place. Then he quotes an ancient hymn that describes the condition of being in the grasp of that power—death: "Awake! Sleeper! Rise from the dead and Christ shall give you light."

Later, as his letter ends (Eph. 6:10–17), he admonishes the faithful to be strong in the Lord so as to stand against the temptations of the devil. He reminds us that we are not fighting against a material force of flesh and blood but rather against spiritual powers, principalities, the masters of the world who rule in darkness. To ward off its massive power, he instructs us that we need the whole armor of God to stand against it.

In Col. 1:13 Paul reminds us that God the Father has released us from the power of the darkness and transferred us to the kingdom of light which is his Son. In 1 Thess. 5:4–7, he again points out that we have been rescued from the darkness and should not be caught unawares when the light of the truth might come upon us.

DISCOVERING THE INNER OTHER

Clearly, the concept of a power that is out to destroy every human soul takes up a considerable amount of room in the Christian religious tradition. What is the meaning of this demonic force that seems to be a universal power, constantly working over and within every human soul? What do we, as "modern," "scientific" people do with this concept of a demonic power to align it with our rationality?

Some years ago, I sat listening to a client. At a certain point, while relating a troublesome event to me, she stopped referring to herself as "I" and began referring to herself in the second person, as "you." I was puzzled by that shift. It was as though there were someone else addressing her from inside her own being, from inside her own Self. At the same time, it was outside her.

The pattern of this grammatical shift revealed a harsh, unsatisfiable critic that questioned my client's every move, denigrating any decision she might even consider making: "Why do you want to do that? That's stupid!" Or it would order her about in a very demeaning way: "Well, as soon as you get up, you're going to have to write all those letters and get the house in order before you do anything else! What do you mean you just want to relax? Who do you think you are? You'd better get moving!"

I pointed out to her the pattern I was discerning. Initially, she was surprised by my observation. However, when I asked her what was going on inside her when I was hearing the "voice" that spoke to her as a "you," it didn't take her long to paint a powerful picture of the inner world where all this was happening.

She said it was as though there were a presence, a being "in the back of her head" (she actually pointed to the back of her head) that spoke to her in a crude and rude manner. It was constantly attacking her, putting her down, making her feel as though she were nothing. Her description had a powerful impact on me and made a great deal of sense.

I began to listen for this phenomenon in the other people with whom I worked. Similar patterns began to emerge; many of them had also had inner "voices" who spoke out loud with abuse and disrespect. When I pointed out what I was hearing and asked them to tell me what was happening, I got responses that were similar to the woman with whom I had first noticed the phenomenon: "It's like there's this voice in the back of my head telling me what to do, putting me down if I don't do it just right." "It calls me a fool." "It tells me I'm nothing but a piece of garbage." "There's one part of me that's always criticizing me and it's never satisfied. There's another part of me that's always angry about the criticism— and I can't seem to do anything about that inner argument."

The one thing all these people seemed to agree on is that this "voice" that spoke to them from inside their heads made almost any task impossible to perform with peace and success. It would attack and tear down any anticipated decision, even one as simple as whether or not to get out of bed in the morning. There could be no "right" decision in the face of this harsh inner critic; therefore all decisions seemed a waste of time. To some people, the voice was so intimidating that it became impossible to make any decision because of the overwhelming fear of making a mistake.

As I reflected on the ever increasing pervasiveness of this inner voice in the internal lives of my clients, I discovered my own harsh inner critic as well. I call this internal power the Inner Other. I decided on that name because, although it seems to exist within the psyche of the individual, it addresses the Self as a "you" and seems to stand outside the Self. It is inside the psyche, but it is not inside the Self.

Although this inner power is separate and distinct from the Self, it is created by the Self. Once created, however, this Inner Other seems to have a life all its own with which the individual has a very powerful psychological and emotional relationship.

GIFT BECOMES TYRANT

The Inner Other is like the Trojan Horse. As we discovered in Part I, the Inner Other is created to help a child develop his own identity in relation to the important others in his environment. Initially, the Inner Other comes as a gift: it serves to keep the Self safe from destruction by preventing the loss of love of the child's important others.

However, when the Self wakes up in adulthood, it finds that it has been taken over by the dark and evil contents that had been hidden in the belly of the gift. Now the gift has turned into an enemy that inhabits the very center of the city of the Self.

It has become the enemy because the Self can no longer be its Self but rather must conform to an image dictated to it by the Inner Other. Freud called this part of the psyche the Super Ego, which literally means from the Latin, "that which stands over the Self." This Super Ego, then, becomes an inner tyrant who towers over the parts of the Self that are stuck back in childhood, ordering them to be other than who they are. In other words, the law of the Inner Other dictates a loss of identity to the Self.

THE POWER OF THE DARKNESS AND THE INNER OTHER

As I have reflected on the parallels over the years between the Inner Other and the power of darkness of the Scripture, the list of similarities has grown. Here are ten of them:

1. Universality

The most powerful characteristic shared by the power of darkness and the Inner Other is their universality in the human experience. When we read the Gospel of John or the writings of Paul, the power of darkness is always implicitly or explicitly regarded as part of the human experience: this inner power of darkness is intrinsic to the human condition.

The Inner Other is also intrinsic to the human experience. To begin with, it is an essential part of the human developmental process. In order for the emerging child-person to become individuated within the context of the human social situation, the child *has to* create an Inner Other. Once created, the Inner Other becomes a permanent, active fixture that functions within the psyche of every human adult to a greater or lesser extent, depending on the circumstances of child-hood. Therefore, the Inner Other is most definitely an intrinsic part of the human experience.

2. The Inner Power of Sin

In Romans 7, Paul talks about a power that resides within him, which he calls the power of sin, and which causes him great confusion. It tricks him into doing the very thing he hates (v. 15). The good that he wants to do is vetoed by this same power and he ends up doing the evil he would not otherwise do (v. 19). He is seduced into the kind of sin that causes him to miss the point of God's benevolent design for him.

Paul says that he does not understand his own behavior because he does the things that contradict his sense of right and wrong, and they happen in ways over which he seems to have little or no control. He is confused about what is happening to him under those circumstances.

The power of the Inner Other has the same effect. When people come to me for help, they, like Paul, are confused by what is happening to them. They too respond to events and behave in ways that are surprising and even abhorrent to them. They don't know where these responses come from and they seem to have little or no control over them. Some of the feelings that generate this confusion are unexplained rage, fear, anxiety, worthlessness, loneliness, guilt, shame, and the like. Some typical thoughts that underlie the confusion are "Nobody likes me," "I can't do anything right (or well enough)," or "I'm unimportant." Beneath those thoughts and feelings are: "You idiot! What did you do that for?! You're going to look like a fool when people see what you did!" Or, "If you show people what you're feeling (sad, angry, fearful, and so on), people aren't going to respect you, and then you'll feel really bad. So just swallow it and make as though nothing is happening to you. Put on a good face and it will all be okay."

When these kinds of feelings, thoughts or behaviors emerge from that inner place, the Self is clouded in darkness, compromised by those inner processes and left in great confusion, not knowing where all of this is coming from and seemingly helpless to do anything about it. The Inner Other causes its subject to be other than who they are instead of being who they are in the image and likeness of God. And like Paul, those who are strangled by its grip cry out: "Oh! What a wretched person I am! Who will rescue me from this power that makes my life so black and empty?"

3. Inner But Other

As Paul ponders how this power operates in his life, he concludes that when it is in operation, it is no longer he who is in charge, but rather the power who has charge over him (v. 20). So in a sense, this power that overtakes him is not him, but something that exists separate and distinct from his own being, even though it dwells within him.

As he examines this power, he sees it as a law separate and in contradiction to the law of God. Although his will is turned to the rightness of the law of God, this power interrupts his ability to follow that law and rules him through its own set of laws that pollutes his being and makes him captive to its power.

Likewise, the Inner Other stands outside the conscious being of the Self, nagging it, putting it down, denigrating it, rendering it worthless, empty, and helpless. It discounts the worth and beauty of being in the image and likeness of God and sets up its own set of "laws." Thus, the individual who is in the power of its darkness finds himself lost to his own identity and therefore to the law of God.

4. Loss of Self-Empowerment

There are many instances in the Scriptures when the power of darkness that Paul describes is in force, and an individual is possessed by demons and no longer in charge of his Self. When Jesus casts the demon(s) out, a profound change comes over the person. Where there once was a "madman" who could make no connections with those around him, there now stands a *person* who is able to spread the word of God (Luke 8:36–39). The person has regained control of his identity.

The loss of Self-empowerment is one of the most significant symptoms of an individual whose being has been taken over by her Inner Other. What renders those of us who are under its dominion helpless is that the Inner Other persona eats away at any positive Self-image that we might have, beating up on us whenever we transgress any one of its multitude of rules or whenever we fail to live up to its perfectionistic demands. It serves as a wedge by which the Self is split into disparate parts which are stuck back in childhood, standing helpless before this internal monster. As children, whenever we sensed our Selves out of favor with our important others, we felt ashamed, guilt-ridden, inadequate, worthless, empty, helpless and victimized.

Most of the time the conscious, adult Self knows that these kinds of thoughts, feelings and experiences are not true representations of reality, but the parts of the Self that are buried in the unconscious do not. What the conscious Self knows does not seem to allay these deep fears. This deep, unconscious war within the psyche permeates the entire Self. The shame, guilt, worthlessness, emptiness, inadequacy, helplessness, and sense of failure and rage seem to rule us in spite of our contrary cognitive conscious knowledge.

The inner despair that accompanies these feelings and perceptions about the Self makes it difficult—sometimes impossible—to function at all. Standing before our internal monster, we are unable to experience our Selves empowered over our own lives. This echoes Paul's sense of loss of identity and empowerment when he faces the Power of Sin within him.

5. Spiritual and Physical Tortures

The tremendous inner torture of the demon-possessed, the pain inflict-
ed on their minds and bodies, seems to accurately describe the torments
of many of the people with whom I've worked over the years. Paul's
confusion in Romans 7 about the inner power that takes him over, seduc-
ing, tricking, and manipulating him into doing the very things he would
not do if "he were in his right mind," and his plaintive cry of wretched-
ness at being captured by this power, bring to mind all that I have witnessed over and over again when people find themselves in the thralls of
their Inner Other.

These pains and torments are not limited to the realm of the mind.
In Mark 9:14–29, there is an account of a young boy possessed by a spirit that renders him dumb, seizes him and dashes him to the ground. The
spirit causes the boy to grind his teeth, foam at the mouth, and go entirely rigid; sometimes the spirit casts the boy into the fire or the water so that
the father fears for his son's life. When Jesus commands the spirit to leave
the boy, his symptoms disappear.

These images of pain and physical torture remind me very much of
the physical "tortures" and self-destructive behavior I witness in my clients
day after day: the woman who passed out in her bathroom, was severely
injured and recovered only to have a terrible automobile accident a week
later; the young man who became rigid and dumb, and who, while he was
in a catatonic state, remembers his inner voice saying to him, "We've got
you now!"; a woman who suffered esophageal collapse and chronic, debilitating diarrhea; a woman who was in traction for six months because of
chronic neck and back pain; another whose jaw and neck ached constantly
from the grinding of her teeth; countless ulcers, colitis, chronic colds,
infections, and muscular pain. Yet when these people came to recognize
the real presence of their inner demons within them and exorcise themselves of these demons, their symptoms, too, disappeared.

6. Lies, Tricks, and Half Truths

How do these demons come to command a young boy's body? How
does the power of darkness overtake Paul's soul? In the story told earlier in this chapter of Jesus' temptations in the desert, an essential device
of the dark one is revealed: the use of half-truths, tricks and lies to seduce
an unwary individual into its orbit of power. When Satan taunts Jesus to
turn stones to loaves of bread and when it dares Jesus to throw himself
off the roof of the temple, it purposely uses (and misinterprets) God's

own words to fit its devious ends in an attempt to seduce Jesus into the trap of its power.

The Inner Other manipulates the individual soul in the same way. It creates half-truths that we come to believe as real. One of the most powerful half-truths is the Inner Other's assertion that it knows us better than we know our Selves. Because it was formulated at the very earliest stages of our consciousness, there are parts of our Self that believe the "secrets"the Inner Other claims it knows about us. One of these "secrets" is that we are worthless. We all come out of childhood believing this to a certain extent, and the Inner Other is the vehicle by which this belief is maintained.

With that as the starting point, the Inner Other then utters other terrifying half-truths and lies: "You can't do anything right. You're nothing but a big failure—that proves that you're worthless! You'd better be careful. If you let people see how imperfect you are, they won't like you. Then think how you'll feel!" Because these beliefs are so deep-seated and firmly rooted, we buy into the half-truths and lies, and then we are within the power of the Inner Other.

7. I Will Give You All, If You Worship Me

There is one further temptation Satan lays before Jesus: worship me, it promises, and all the kingdoms of the world and all its glory shall belong to you. The Inner Other also demands worship and makes promises of prosperity and glory: worship me, it promises, do everything I tell you to do, and I will help you hide the ugly truth about yourself; otherwise you will always be a failure and an outcast.

8. My Name Is Legion, for We Are Many

In my first book, *Healing the Fractured Self*, I traced how a client I called Dana had incorporated three separate Inner Other voices, who were imaged after her mother, her father, and her great aunt. The activity of these inner voices tore her apart and made the simple act of getting out of bed in the morning a task equivalent to climbing Mount Everest. The following excerpts from a therapy session with Dana depict the kind of struggle she had every day. On this particular day, she was caught in the vise of a dilemma. She needed to go shopping but the attack of her Inner Other voices so debilitated her she didn't know if she could go, so she decided to stay home. She felt overwhelmed by what was happening inside her. She pleaded with her husband Bob to stay home with her because she was feeling so vulnerable to inner attack. Bob did stay home, and even that backfired against her. As you read her description of what was happening to her, keep two things in mind:

1. Notice how she keeps shifting from "I " to "you" as the different internalized voices address her and she responds to them in argument.

2. As you read what she is going through, you may very well feel confused. Your sense of confusion mirrors the confusion that Dana herself experienced as she lived through this. These feelings of confusion occur because the commands and countermands being shouted at her from inside are indeed contradictory. Any decision she might make would be "wrong." It is this very confusion that immobilized her.

DANA: Bob stayed home . . . and was distressed about it. And I was distressed too. Yet, I wanted him to be there! So there *you* were, mixed up. Good spot to be in, right? "Don't go shopping! *You're* going to be sick in the store." But I went, and I didn't get sick in the store. Do I have to fight every battle? "What do *you* want to go to therapy for? So exhausting!"

(Later in the session)

I'm not strong when I'm sick. I shake. I keep telling myself, "I'm not sick!" And then again, *"You* must be sick, if *you* feel that way. *You* don't want to get out of bed in the morning. *You* must be sick, *you* don't have anything to live for!" You keep telling me I do! And you can control me if I'm sick. There must be another world besides this one. Another life.

(Still later in the session)

If *you* had gone to work, *you* wouldn't have a pain in *your* stomach. Guilty! "I'm not guilty! Stop twisting me around!" "Don't go to therapy; *you're* not getting anywhere. *You're* wasting *your* time. *You* don't do what *you're* told. *You* don't try hard enough. What's Jack going to say when he sees *you*? *You're* not getting anywhere after all this time."

No wonder Dana was confused and immobilized! The "you" voice that beckoned her back to bed was the Mother-Demon voice who promised her love if she were in bed, sick. The "you" voice that called her "guilty" was her Great-Aunt-Demon attacking her because she was faking an illness to get Mommy's attention (as she did during childhood). The "you" voice that said she wasn't trying hard enough was her Inner Father, who represented her real father yelling at her over her arithmetic homework.

The result was that Dana was caught in an internal tug-of-war. If she was to get love, she must fall ill, flee to bed and call out to her husband to minister to her, just as she had called out to her mother in childhood. In doing so, however, she became subject to her Great-Aunt-Demon's charges of malingering. Then her Internal Father would step into the bedroom and yell at her because she wasn't trying hard enough.

This inner attack by the group of dark inner voices and the effect it had on her bring to mind the story in the Scriptures of the man who lived among the tombs (Mark 5:1–20). He was possessed by an unclean spirit who had him so agitated and out of control that he could no longer be bound, even with chains. He was all bruises and sores because day and night he went about crying and hitting himself with stones.

When he spots Jesus, he runs to him, bows down in worship and cries, "What do you want of me, Son of the Most High?"

Jesus tells the spirit to leave the man. But it responds, begging him not to torture it. Jesus asks its name, and it replies, "My name is Legion, for we are many." It asks Jesus not to send them away altogether but to send them into a nearby herd of swine. Jesus does this, and the swine stampede over a cliff, fall into the sea and are drowned.

This story confirms the parallel between the psychological process I witness in my clients and the symbolic language of the Gospel stories. Clearly, Dana had more than one voice torturing her. Because these voices contradicted each other, she was torn apart trying to conform to what they told her to do. Her voices, too, were legion, and they left her psychologically bruised and sore as she tried to get free of their chains.

9. Resistance

This pain and torture is described over and over again in the writings of John and Paul. But the Scripture also points out that, in spite of the pain we suffer at the hand of the power of sin, we still choose the darkness over the light, and fight to remain in its domain.

So, too, for those who are ruled by the Inner Other. It is incredibly difficult for most people to give up their attachment to their inner voices. People cry, just as Paul did, "Oh, what a miserable wretch I am!" Then they fight to hang on to the Inner Other with every ounce of energy they have. Some people actually leave the therapeutic process because they are unwilling to give up the "security" of the Inner Other, even though they are able, at one level, to recognize what that inner being does to their life. Further, it's precisely this resistance to giving up the Inner Other's rule over the Self that often causes therapy to be such a long, excruciating experience. If it were easier for people to let go, the process could be shortened considerably.

10. Not Knowing the Law, I Did Not Know Sin

In Rom. 7:7–12, Paul says that if he had not known the Law, he would not have known sin. For instance, knowing that the Law says "Thou shalt not covet," not only makes him aware of the Law, but incites him to covetousness as well. The commandment that was supposed to lead him to life, led instead to his "death." Instead of bringing him to an unfolding of who he was, it resulted in closing him down to who he was.

For each of us, prior to the time that we are ready to create our Inner Other, we exist in a state of innocence to wrongdoing. However, once we are ready to establish that entity within our psyche, we become aware that others exist apart from our Selves. We also become aware that they have rights and boundaries that we intrude upon, and we are held progressively responsible for these intrusions as we grow up. Although the Inner Other's proper function was to assist us in knowing the height, breadth and depth of our boundaries in relationship to others, as we have seen, this inner entity backfires and erodes us from within.

Thus, in a very real way, the Inner Other begins as a knowledge of the law that is supposed to help us appreciate our own being in relationship to others. But like the Law that Paul speaks of, this inner law becomes distorted and twisted within us and, instead of helping us live according to the will of God, it works against that divine purpose.

The Law that Paul had used as the reference point for his life before his reformation was the Law of the Old Testament that had been handed down from the Prophets and Fathers of Israel. Like the law of the Inner Other, its original purpose was to lead the People of Israel along the path to YHWH. But, again like the law of the Inner Other, it had become distorted and twisted and no longer led the People to the light. Instead, it led them into darkness.

The Law had made that transformation because it too had become contaminated by the human reality of the Inner-Other-Demon. Although it had been communicated to the people of Israel by God, they had lost God's Spirit because it had become filtered though the energy of the power of darkness, the Inner Other. The Law had become an externalization of the internal law of the Inner Other.

Once Jesus the Christ came and revealed the true meaning of the Law, Paul (and others) were confronted with the sin that it had brought upon them. So, too, are we confronted with the distortion of the true purpose of our existence by our internalized power of darkness, the Inner Other, when it is brought up against the light of Christ's revelation.

RESPONSIBILITY: DEFENSE AGAINST THE POWER

The power of these internal demons seems to be overwhelming. Do we, as mere mortals, have any defense against them? When we claim the Law of God, Paul tells us, their power will be vanquished. As he ponders over the battle that rages within him, he cries out, "How wretched am I! Who will deliver me from the pain and spiritual death of this conflict?" His answer is Jesus, the Christ, who is the Lord! It is the Christ that brings him back to the Law of God and vision of God's will for him, to live in the image and likeness of God.

Paul comes to realize that he is not to lie down passively before this dark power, letting it take him over. Rather, he asserts that he must take the responsibility as to whether he is ruled by the law of God or the law of sin (vs. 25).

Likewise, for those who are being destroyed by their Inner Others, the only defense is to claim back their identity. When they do that, they give up the law of the Inner Other, the core of which is to be other than who I am. Only by reclaiming his own uniqueness and individuality can the Self come back to life and live in the light of God his Creator.

The grip the Inner Other has on the human reality is immense. The power of Satan is awesome. The way both overtake the soul is remarkably parallel. After considering all the similarities between the power of darkness, Satan and the demonic as they are revealed in the Scripture, and the Inner Other as it has revealed itself in the lives of the clients with whom I have worked, I have come to the conclusion that they are one and the same. What the Bible refers to as Satan we can understand in psychological terms as the Inner Other.

THE RATIONAL VS. THE RELIGIOUS

Bringing together this being who is called Inner Other, Super Ego, and Internal Parent in the realm of psychology, and Evil Spirit, Demon, Prince of Darkness, and Satan in the realm of theology and mythology, does not in any way diminish the power or significance of this being in either realm.

To the "liberated" modern mind, the idea that there are evil spirits in the world is usually dismissed and thought of as magical and medieval. To the "religious" mind, denying the world of evil spirits and demons is to dismiss the importance of things spiritual and is often thought to verge on heresy. To these two ways of thinking, I would like to offer another viewpoint.

To the modern, rationalistic way of thinking, I would like to say that there are many ways in which a problem may be approached. Although the medievalist, the person(s) who created the Garden myth, or even Jesus himself, did not possess the "scientific" method and the language that goes along with it, that does not mean they did not appreciate, realize and articulate the problem in a vocabulary and grammar that spoke in some way to the common understanding. Although the language of modern psychology may shed new light on an old problem, or it might bring a focus never before possible, it remains the same phenomenon approached in other "languages."

To the religious person, I would like to say that bringing the psychological understanding of the forces that bring darkness into our lives does not need to dilute or undermine the religious belief system in any way. Quite to the contrary, keeping the concept of demons and evil spirits cloaked in a mysterious, untouchable nether world, undermines the concept of evil demons by attributing their activity to the unseen, magical and nonspecific. That makes evil incomprehensible and unmanageable in the normal flow of life.

THE REALNESS OF THE DEMONIC

To overcome the evil one, we must count on the full power of God to stand behind us (Rom. 8:31–39). Jesus Christ came to give witness to the sanctity of each and every individual soul. The powers of darkness within and around us do not want this God-message to be heard. Their powers are amassed against its being heard, for it is they who murdered the God-incarnate in the person of Jesus.

But as each of us struggles, as Jesus the Christ did, to resist their message of darkness, we can fall back on his witness to God's faithfulness to us. From that, we can draw the strength to overcome our own Satan, the powerful Inner Other that tries to take over our Self and make it over into its own likeness, which is darkness and emptiness. The true God, however, wants something else for us—that we exist in the light in which we were created.

≪7≫

Demons Incarnate: The Religious Leaders as Personifications of the Inner Other

A METAPHOR: THE POWER WITHIN

The powers of darkness are constantly battling with and around us to "murder" God's message to us. When Jesus lived on Earth, the powers of darkness were manifested in some of the leaders of the Jewish religious structure—those who so adamantly opposed Jesus the Christ.

Who were they? They were men immersed in their own toxic shame and guilt, who had devised a "religious" system that they thought would somehow bring them some relief from these deep, painful feelings. They created a system of ritualistic practices they thought could "buy off" their internal persecutors (whom they thought were the real God). They thought that by "keeping up appearances," by following an elaborate system of laws and traditions, they could ease their toxic guilt and shame.

This is something we all do, guided (or misguided) by our Inner Other: we think that by concentrating on how we appear to others and by appearing to be other than who we are, we can get rid of the toxic shame and guilt generated by the Inner Other. But all that does is momentarily push the shame and guilt to one side, only to have it seep back in again.

For example, there is a story in Matthew (12:1–15) where Jesus and his disciples are walking through a grain field on the Sabbath. The disciples, being hungry, pluck some of the grain and begin to eat. The Pharisees (one of the political parties within the power elite) criticize them for plucking grain on the Sabbath. Later, they criticize Jesus for healing a cripple on the Sabbath. Jesus' response is to ask who among them, if he had a son fall in a well on the Sabbath, would not save him? What he is really asking is which is more important, to obey the letter of the law, or to respond to human need?

But the Pharisees are not convinced. They ". . . went out and took counsel against him, how to destroy him" (Matt. 12:14). They choose to cling to their beliefs in the customs that keep intact their posture of guilt and shame before the God-Parent. They buy so completely into this system that they, in a very real sense, become their Inner Others.

By giving themselves over so completely to the demonic system, their identities are "erased" and the demonic persona becomes their identity. When they then attempt to impose that system onto the faithful of the Jewish community, they behave toward the faithful the way our demons relate to us from within.

Furthermore, referring to them, Jesus says, "Any one who commits sin is a slave to it. Being slaves, you will be displaced by me, the Son. I can make you free, but you seek to kill me because you cannot find a place within you for the word I speak. I speak to you of what I have seen from the Holy Parent but you do what you hear from your parent. You do not understand what I say because you cannot bear to hear it. *You are of your father, who is the Devil, and you will to do his will.* He was a murderer from the beginning of time. There is no truth in him. It is his very nature to lie, as he is the creator of lies. So when I reveal the truth, you cannot believe me. Whoever is of God hears the word of God. But you cannot hear those words because you are not of God" (John 8:34–59).

Thus, Jesus names these men for who they are. He tells them (and us) what they symbolize: the external, visible, tangible personifications of the Inner-Other-Demon.

By studying how Jesus reacts to the religious leaders' continued investment in the shame-and-guilt system of relating to God, and their attempts to keep the people of Israel bound up in that system, we see how Jesus regarded the system itself.

As we examine and observe Jesus' reactions, we can begin to understand his response to the power that attempts to keep us enslaved through toxic guilt and shame. Through his responses to it we can also begin to understand how we our Selves can stop being the victim of this inner force, and that God is on our side in this internal conflict.

THE DEMONIC LAWS

As we observe these men of darkness, we learn about the demonic law according to which they operate. How these men function, having been taken over so completely by their demonic forces, gives us insight as to how the demonic power preys upon us from within our own being. By contrast, we will also see how Jesus responds to these old laws and gives us a new one to live by.

Appearances

In Matt. 15:1–18, the Pharisees confront Jesus about not conforming to their tradition of washing one's hands before one eats. Jesus replies that instead of honoring God through tradition and Scripture, they honor their own darkness. He says that it is not what goes into the mouth that defiles a person, but what comes out of the mouth; that which comes out of the mouth proceeds from the heart, and this is what defiles a person. "For out of the heart come evil thoughts . . ." (Matt. 15:1–18).

What is the evil that comes out of their mouths from the depths of their hearts?

The powers who rule us from within would have us believe that what saves us in the eyes of God is that we live up to appearances. Jesus is declaring that this religious framework is *against* the order of God and destructive to the individual who adheres to it, for, although it promises to save life, it only destroys it. Not only does Jesus warn against that way of thinking, he condemns the powers that seduce us into it because they keep us poisoned with guilt and shame, and rob us of the beauty and goodness that exist in the image of God.

Jesus warns his disciples that the Pharisees—and by extension, our inner demons—are evil and faithless, that they want our souls. Jesus, in concern for us in our IAM-ness, asks what good it would do to listen to them, thereby gaining the whole world but, in the process, killing your Self and losing your soul (Matt. 16:1–12, 26).

GUILT AND SHAME

If the power of darkness is so harmful to us, how does it maintain its hold over us? By generating guilt and shame within us if we do not conform to its system. Jesus tells a story that powerfully outlines this system of guilt and shame. It is one of a king who decides to collect on all the debts due him (Matt. 18:23–35). It is a story of being owed and owing, the focal point to any system of toxic guilt and shame:

> One of the servants in particular owes the king a great deal of money, which he cannot pay. The king threatens to sell him, his wife, his children and all their possessions in order to collect his due. But the servant begs for mercy, and the king, in pity for him, releases him from his debt.

On his way out of the Hall, the servant comes upon a fellow servant who owes *him* money. Although the man begs for mercy, the servant demands his money and sends his friend to jail for nonpayment.

In this story, the servant is ruled by toxic guilt and shame. He cannot accept the king's forgiveness, and through his treatment of the second servant, finds a way to remain in the king's debt and be punished for it.

The king in this story is a metaphor for the Heavenly Father and the servant is a metaphor for the religious leaders. The Holy, Creator God is willing to forgive any debt, out of generosity, compassion and kindness. The servant, however, who is ruled by the powers of darkness, is unable to accept forgiveness. Therefore, he "acts out" by being unable to forgive the second servant. When the king discovers the servant's mistreatment of the second man, he holds him accountable. The King is so angered that he casts the servant into prison until he pays what he owes.

The God Jesus represents is a very different God than the one portrayed in the Garden story. The God in the Garden story functions out of toxic guilt and shame, with all kinds of expectations based on obligation and owing. The God revealed by Jesus is one of unconditional love. He doesn't need to prove anything about his own worth—therefore, His love is given without agenda. And, as is shown in this story, God is unhappy with those who mistreat others through toxic guilt and shame and represent Him as being unforgiving. Thus, any power, internal or external, that attempts to rule the IAM through toxic guilt and shame is considered by God to be a violator of His will and is to be held accountable.

I Am Unequal

The Inner Other devalues us by maintaining a Self-image immersed in guilt and shame. It does this by making us believe we are less than everyone else in the world. Jesus tells a story to release us of this terrible burden (Matt. 20:1–16).

There was a vineyard owner who hired workers at the beginning of the day and agreed to a sum they would receive for their work. As each quarter of the day passed, he hired more workers. When the day ended, the workers lined up, first to last. The landlord paid everyone the same sum he had promised the original workers—no matter how many hours each man had actually worked. When this happened, the men who had worked all day began to grumble and complain. The landlord responded by saying that he was doing them no wrong. He was paying what they agreed upon and he asks them why they reproach him for being generous.

Because we perceive our Selves as being less than everyone else, we become jealous that everyone else is getting "a better deal" in life than we are. We anxiously look around for the ways others are better, and thus invest a great deal of energy in comparing and complaining and trying to catch up to those who are "better." When we enter into that system, we have been hoodwinked into believing our demons. The energy that could have been used in growth is, instead, used to stay in the orbit of darkness of the Evil One.

The Inner Other tries to convince us that we are of little value in the order of creation, and that everyone else is of infinitely greater value than our Selves. As a result, it seduces us into thinking that everyone deserves more in value than our Selves. The result is that we view our Selves as insignificant and worthless.

Through the story of the king and the servant, however, Jesus is saying that we are all of equal worth in the eyes of God. Any entity that tries to rob us of that essential experience of our Selves will have to face the reproach of the Lord. The Lord loves us all; that is His generosity. The sanctity of who we are in the imaged likeness of God is reaffirmed.

Dependency

By getting us to adhere to their system of guilt and shame, the Inner Powers force us into a relationship of dependency with them. They require us to keep referring to them as the mediators between our Selves and God. The result is that we cannot be free to be our own person in relationship with God. Within their system, we are told to believe that guilt and shame before God are intrinsic to our very being. These powers determine what appeases God; therefore they tell us when and how the guilt and shame can be temporarily removed to allow a direct connection with God. This, however, makes us dependent on them to validate our sense of worth and identity. Without them, we cannot "exist"; we cannot be in the autonomy of our IAM-ness.

So why not eliminate the middlemen? The people of God would then have a free relationship with Him, autonomous from these dark figures. Through the witness of Jesus as the Son of God, God is declaring this type of guilt and shame relationship with Him as invalid. Instead, we are to be in direct union with the Lord through the fullness of our IAM. Thus, one of the essential characters of the IAM qualities is restored to us.

No Mistakes Allowed

The last demonic law says "no mistakes allowed." To make a mistake means to be imperfect. Imperfection means there is a flaw in the soul, which generates toxic shame. Making a mistake also means I have failed others, which yields toxic guilt. Making a mistake, thereby revealing one's imperfection and shamefulness, becomes so toxic it seems to be worthy of death.

There was a woman who was caught in adultery. The scribes and Pharisees dragged her to Jesus ready to execute her. They challenged Jesus to "keep the law," hoping to trap him. If he "keeps the law," he is one of them. If not, he demonstrates he is not of God. So they said to him, "Moses said to stone whosoever is found to be in adultery. What do you say about this?"

Jesus stooped down and drew doodles in the dust. Finally, he looked up and said," Whosoever among you is without sin, cast the first stone." Then he bent down again and continued his doodles. One by one, his challengers turned away. Left alone with the woman, he looked up and said to her, "Where have they all gone?" "They left," she replied. "None of them have condemned you, so neither will I," said Jesus (John 8:2–11).

It is this intolerance of mistakes by the demon-force that eats away at the hearts and minds of humankind. It is this tactic that keeps people like Dana in a constant state of fear, isolation and emptiness. Once the mistake is manifest, the demon is merciless in its attack.

The mistake takes on more value than the person; because of the mistake, the demon demands the person be put to death. It is this type of hypercriticism from within that plummets people into profound depression; catatonia (a complete immobility from fear of making a mistake); illnesses ranging from ulcers to "unconscious" suicide through diseases like cancer; to premeditated, conscious suicide.

Jesus, however, refutes this harsh criticism. His response tells us that mistakes, even serious ones, are not the worst things in the world. They certainly do not mean the death of the individual who has blundered into one, nor do they mean that the person has been rendered worthless.

KNOWING WHO THEY ARE

These were the laws under which the religious leaders operated. Comprehending what the religious leaders represent helps us understand how the power of darkness operates. Through this understanding, we can see how Jesus moves toward its destruction, eventually giving us power over it as well.

❧8❧

Possession

I Am Because You Are

To understand how the evil one rules us so profoundly through toxic guilt and shame, we need to examine the original process of possession that occurs in each one of us. We began this examination in chapter two. In this chapter, we'll take an in-depth look at what this process is, how it's maintained within us, and how it keeps the evil one in power over us.

As various skills (the ability to crawl, then walk; the use of language; the manipulation of objects) develop, a child becomes increasingly aware that others are not mere extensions of his Self, but exist independently of him. It is probably at this point that the first inklings of Self-awareness, the IAM-ness, begin to manifest themselves to the child.

This Self-awareness is hazy and undefined; a sense of worth, identity, uniqueness and autonomy from others does not happen in a single flash. It builds over a relatively long period of time through a complex psycho-developmental process that, even under the best of circumstances, is not completed until the end of adolescence. Until these attributes of IAM-ness are established, the IAM-ness itself is weak, vulnerable and fragile.

Take, for example, an infant playing with his mother in the nursery. The child crawls out of the room, leaving his mother behind. What happens if the child returns to the room and his mother is no longer there? He will invariably become very upset, usually screaming at the top of his lungs. The "disappearance" of the mother causes the child to perceive his own identity as being in jeopardy.

At this stage, the child's identity is fused with his parent's. This is precisely what the child is coming to terms with when he plays the game of peek-a-boo. As he covers his eyes, the person out there "disappears." What the child discovers, and begins to work through in this game, is that visual disappearance does *not* mean the actual evaporation of the other. That's why this game results in great delight and squeals of pleasure. The child discovers that the "other" really does stick around even though the he cannot see her. This discovery allows the separation from parental figures, especially the mother, to begin in earnest.

I Am Because I Am Loved

To achieve a solid sense of IAM-ness that is rooted in Self-worth, uniqueness and autonomy, a child needs positive acceptance and approval through his parents' words and actions. This acceptance and approval advance and bolster the Self-image the child is struggling so hard to achieve.

Although the child's sense of identity and Self-awareness is becoming more solid, his sense of Self-value is still nebulous. The major vehicle by which the child gives himself value is by attaching his Self onto the "coat tails" of the parent. The child's "logic" tells him, "By my Self, I don't matter . . . I don't have value. The only person(s) who has value is Mommy (Daddy). I have value because Mommy (Daddy) has value. As long as I am connected to them, I have value." In order for the child to feel good about and to attribute a sense of positive value to his Self, a sense of connection to a "good" parent is extremely important. So, when a child receives positive acceptance and approval from the important other(s), he experiences his IAM-ness and his sense of worth as established, enhanced and growing.

On the other hand, if the parenting figure (necessarily or unnecessarily) disapproves of the child, the sense of value the child places in his IAM-ness is diminished. Disapproval is experienced by the child as a devaluation of his Self, and becomes a statement of "badness" in the child's understanding of his Self. Thus, the child's logic tells him, "If my parent says I am bad, then IAM bad."

When a young child experiences this disapproval, he experiences a primal and primitive sense of shame and guilt. In fact, it is necessary that the child experience this form of shame and guilt if he is violating the rights and boundaries of others or is endangering his Self. This sense of shame and guilt is critical and essential to the child's socialization. It is through this awareness of shame and guilt that the child begins to learn that the universe is not his private toy entirely at his disposal. Without this sense of shame and guilt, the child would become a psychopathic adult.

The negative response of the parent is, then, experienced by the child as a threat to his psychological well being. Because of the importance of the acceptance and approval of the important others in maintaining a positive IAM state in the quality of Self-worth, the child strives to maintain or reinstate his Self into the good graces of the important other. To assist him in this effort, the child has at his disposal the psychological ability to create an internal image of his parent approving or disapproving of his behavior.

THE BALANCING ACT

For instance, when a young child passes through the "no" stage, what she is really saying is, "I am separate from you; I can be different from you by saying 'no' to you." How well the child crosses from her fused identity with her important others to fully autonomous, Self-identified, unique IAM-ness that contains Self-worth is dependent on the solidity of the bridge she uses to get to the other side; the strength of that bridge depends on how well the parents respond to the child's striving for these psychological qualities.

Eavesdrop on a three-year-old who has just misbehaved and you'll probably hear her tell her teddy bear or imaginary playmate, "You've been a naughty girl!" or "You're a bad boy!" Very often, the child will strike the toy.

I recall an example of this kind of behavior, which occurred some time ago. One afternoon I was entertaining several couples and their children in my home. One of the mothers, whom I shall call Martha, was very anxious about the activity and whereabouts of her four-year-old daughter, whom I shall call Mary. Mary was busily exploring my large apartment. Every few minutes Martha would send her husband or one of the older children down the hall to check on Mary.

I tried to assure Martha that the other rooms in the apartment were all occupied so Mary wouldn't be completely unattended wherever she was. Still, Martha couldn't relax until Mary came back into the room with us. Eventually, Mary settled down at the coffee table with a felt-tipped pen and a piece of paper. She drew quietly until, in an attempt to make dots, she began to use the pen in a way that would destroy the tip. Since it was my pen and I didn't want it ruined, I started to ask Mary not to use the pen that way; I was about to show her a way to make dots without damaging the pen. Before I could say one word, Martha interrupted and, in a sharp tone of voice, said, "Mary, don't do that!" Mary's look of wounded surprise quickly changed to anger. Not more than a minute later, Mary took hold of her favorite doll. She rolled up the sheet of paper and stuck it into the doll's mouth. She then slapped the doll and mimicked her mother's words: "Don't do that! You bad girl!"

What was happening in this event for Mary? The message Mary processed from her interaction with her mother that afternoon had nothing to do with the proper use of a pen. All afternoon, Martha's interaction with her daughter was based on her desire to maintain control of the child. This, of course, had put Mary's spontaneous activity under close scrutiny. Martha's compulsion to monitor Mary at all times during the afternoon (and at other times) communicated to Mary that spontaneity itself was the cause of parental disapproval. All of these controls or limitations were finally summed up for Mary in her mother's statement, "Don't do that!" because it offered no alternatives; it was simply another limitation in response to Mary's spontaneity.

Mary's response was to psychologically disown that part of her Self that had caused her mother's disapproval, and to project it on to her "naughty" doll. In the process, a psychological vacuum was created, which was instantly filled by an internalized image of Martha, the disapproving parent.

When Mary "punished" her doll, and took on the verbal role of her mother, she was acting out her internalized parental image.

There is however, another very important dimension to the process of what was happening to little Mary. Not only did she create an internalized image of her disapproving parent, she also allied her Self with that internalized image.

EVE MADE ME DO IT!

A few years ago, some very good friends of mine called to tell me something they thought I'd find interesting and amusing. They told me that their three-year-old boy, Bobby, had a new playmate. But there was something very different about this playmate—he was invisible and his name was Turkey.

Now, Bobby had a one-year-old sister of whom he was extremely jealous (which was entirely normal). Because of this jealousy, he would act out at times in ways that were inappropriate, disruptive and, if not properly channeled, dangerous. The parents did their best to help the little boy understand what was going on inside of him while at the same time letting him know that some forms of his behavior were not acceptable. But what had now begun to happen was that Bobby would respond to any admonishment by saying, "Turkey made me do it!"

Through this "disowning" process, the child avoids the same radical estrangement from the world of others that is sketched in the Genesis story when Adam and Eve are "expelled" from the Garden. Although Bobby was punished for his misdeeds, in his own mind, he found it necessary to split his Self into "good" or "bad" parts. That way, at least part of his Self avoids the severest of punishments, the complete loss of (or expulsion from) the world of others. Because the "bad" part is disconnected from the "good" part, removed from active service and buried (or imprisoned) within the inner reaches of his psyche, the child believes he has sidestepped the terrible pain he would suffer if he remained whole. However, as we discover when we grow up, this is a deception.

THE ALLY OF THE INNER OTHER

There is a part of the inner dynamic that is not evident here. Another party, also involved in this interplay, needs to be addressed for us to understand this immobilizing and confusing ambiguity.

The follow-up to Bobby's story came a couple of weeks later. Again, I received a telephone call from my friends. This time, though, they were not just passing on an amusing bit of information. They related that earlier in the day, they were in the house and Bobby was in the back yard. All was quiet. Suddenly they heard a blood-curdling scream. With visions of a wounded child and a race to the hospital, they ran to the back door. When they opened it, there was a terrified Bobby, his face streaked with tears. But there wasn't any blood. In confusion and panic, they asked Bobby what was wrong. He said, "Turkey is angry with me and he was chasing me!" They called me because they were greatly disturbed by this event.

Although Bobby may have acted out his feelings from time to time, he himself did not claim them. When his mother says, "You shouldn't have pushed your sister," Bobby's reply is, "I didn't push her. Turkey made me do it." In other words, he's saying, "I'm not angry with her, Turkey is." Bobby won't claim his feelings of anger, thus they never really get resolved. They become encapsulated into an independent persona that takes on its own identity and functions independently of the conscious Self. That is the persona of Turkey (or the Inner Child of Instinct), and he is trapped inside. Because he is trapped, he perceives and regards the part of the Self that put him there as an enemy. Turkey, then, becomes very angry with Bobby.

Bobby, like Mary (and the rest of us), had early on created an internalized parental image. The internal parent had direct access to Bobby, exerting a direct and powerful influence on what Bobby would listen to and take action upon. Turkey, on the other hand, was off in one corner of the psyche, all by himself, isolated and with little access to Bobby. The result is that Turkey experienced himself without any recourse, unheard, always to blame, squashed and suffocated.

When Turkey chased Bobby around the yard, he was telling him in no uncertain terms that this inner political arrangement would not do. It was not a fair fight. It's as if Turkey were saying to Bobby, "I can't win against someone that powerful. I need someone my own size to fight with." Bobby's compromise is to create a second Inner Child, one who allies itself with the Internalized Parent (the Inner Other).

The conflict between Bobby and his Inner Other was so intense, he needed to create a buffer. He did this by splitting his Self into Turkey and the second Inner Child, who could then fight each other, one step removed from both Bobby and the Inner Other.

Turkey and the second Inner Child are on opposite sides. Turkey is rebellious, and does not always want to do what is "right" or "good" or what he is told. On the other hand, the second Inner Child believes that he must conform to the wishes of the Internal Parent, and fears that if he does not, he places the Self in jeopardy.

THE DECISION MAKER

With Turkey and the Child-Allied-with-the-Internal Parent now in place within the unconscious space of the psyche, this means that Bobby himself occupies a new position within this arrangement, and has a new function. Bobby, the part of the Self whom we "know" and with whom we interact, becomes the Central I.

The primary function of the Central I is to navigate the Self (the total Self-aware being of which the Central I and the individual Inner Children are parts) through life. It is the part of the Self that processes feelings and perceptions, makes judgments about what it processes, and then acts upon those judgments. The information it receives come from both external and internal reality. Thus the Central I possesses two "faces."

One face of the Central I, the conscious aspect of the Self that we in the outside world know as Bobby, processes events in the outside world and arrives at ways to react to those events. As long as the Central I is influenced only by the outside world, its interactions are fairly simple and straightforward. That's the easy part.

There is, however, another face of the Central I that observes and interacts with the inner world of the psyche. The psyche, or the unconscious, is comprised of everything we have experienced during our psychological development, as perceived through all the various parts of the Self. When the "ancient history" of an individual is triggered in the context of any given event, life becomes complicated.

It is the Central I's function to listen to what each of the internal personae is communicating to her, decide which one of them she is going to listen to, and act upon that information. It is this process that determines what the behavior of the Self will be at any given moment.

SURVIVAL

So, within the inner world of the psyche, we end up with two camps of Inner Children, the "Turkey" and the "Child-Allied-to-the-Inner-Other." Both camps agree that they are dedicated to the survival of the Self. Where they disagree, however, is in their definition of survival.

The "Turkey" person is the part of the Self that reacts instinctively and immediately to reality. If there is a perception of a violation, "Turkey" feels the anger, and if it were allowed, would get the Central I to respond to the violator.

The Child-Allied-to-the-Inner-Other, on the other hand, perceives his survival as being tied to his bonds with the important others. This part does not react to an event per se; rather his first consideration is what another person will think of his reaction; and this becomes even more important than the actual event.

When either one of these parts of the Self perceives danger, he alerts the Central I to take steps to avoid that danger. If the "Turkey" part is experiencing his life being smothered and "death of identity" approaching, he sends out signals to the Central "I" to do something that will assert that identity. On the other hand, if the Child-Allied-to-the-Inner-Other experiences something that transgresses the "rules," thereby endangering his connectedness with the important other and thus his survival, he will get the Central I to find a way to get out of it, for example, "Turkey made me do it."

Once again, Bobby provides a perfect example. At a party, everyone was gathered around Bobby's little sister, watching her do a little dance. Turkey, feeling ignored and overlooked, urged Bobby to push his sister out of the way. When she fell down, Bobby turned around and said, "Look what happened to her!" as if he had nothing to do with it. So, while Turkey urges Bobby to act out his feelings, the Child-Allied-to-the-Inner-Other urges him to deny it even happened.

Each of these internal actors want to be allowed to determine the reaction to the event so that disaster may be avoided. But from the other's point of view, his warning has not been heeded, and he perceives himself still in jeopardy.

This is a very similar process to the one we find in the Garden story of Genesis (3:10–14) when, after Adam and Eve have eaten of the forbidden fruit, God encounters them "walking" in the garden. They are now Self-aware, conscious of their nakedness and ashamed of it. Because of their shame, they hide their Selves from God. But God calls out to them. When they answer and tell Him they have hidden because of shame, God says, "You have eaten of the forbidden tree, haven't you?" Adam responds, and, pointing the finger at Eve, says, "She gave it to me!" Eve just as quickly turns to the serpent and says, "He talked me into it."

THE POLITICS OF THE MYTH

This is where we return to the Temptation in the Garden myth. The Serpent is Turkey. Adam is the Child-Allied-with-the-Inner-Other. He is the part of the Self who distances himself as much as possible from the transgression. Eve is the Central I who finds herself suspended between the Serpent and the Child-Allied-with-the-Inner-Other. In adult life, she finds that she must listen to both of them and respond to whoever "yells loud enough," warning her that her life is endangered.

When Adam points to Eve, he projects his dangerous "wrongdoing" Self onto the person of Eve. The "parent" (God) turns to Eve and confronts her. She, in turn, as Central I, projects most of the responsibility for her activity onto the Serpent. She does admit she was seduced, thereby avoiding the complete loss of parental love. Thus the Serpent serves the same purpose in this story that the teddy bear, doll, imaginary playmate or pet serves in millions of households all over the world. It is the concrete object onto which the child can project her unwanted Self to deflect the punishment of the angry, disapproving parent. That is how the Inner Child of Instinct (whom Bobby calls "Turkey") is born.

THE DISINTEGRATION OF SELF

There is an incredible irony here. What we are talking about is the formation of the Self. Yet, the child in the act of forming his Self, does so by disintegrating his Self as it is being formed! In other words, even as the child is forming his identity, his sense of uniqueness in the world, that sense of Self-ness is fractured.

Even at the tender age of three, Bobby (and the rest of us) has begun to form a very concrete, operable and active psyche that is peopled with very powerful actors. Bobby apparently understood his parents' reprimands about his inappropriate behavior as condemnations of his feelings of anger, jealousy, frustration. He then split these feelings off as the part of his Self that he identified as jeopardizing his connection with his parents. This part of his Self became Turkey. The rest of him aligned with the now internalized parent that had become his Inner Other.

STRANGULATION

As we get older, our accumulation of experience progressively submerges the Child of Instinct. The Central I, due to societal rules and pressures, usually pays most of his attention to the Child-Allied-to-the-Inner-Other. The Child of Instinct, then, becomes increasingly anxious about its own existence. This anxiety is registered with the Central I. Because the conflict that generates this anxiety is buried in the unconscious, it becomes vague and unspecified. We get mixed messages from our psyche about what to do and not to do, and the Central I becomes increasingly perplexed as he moves from event to event in his life.

Obviously, as long as the Self is fractured and disconnected from himself, there is something radically wrong within. The Self is at war with himself. There is a void where there should be fullness, guilt where there should be peace with the world, worthlessness where there should be value; anxiety where there should be Self-contentment.

THE VIEW FROM ADULTHOOD

As time passes, the personae within the psyche crystallize. Each of them takes on a life all their own. In Bobby's case, this was already happening. The Inner Child of Instinct becomes a distinct entity, usually well hidden from view, occasionally erupting when the demands for his point of view become life-threatening (for instance, when Bobby felt ignored and upstaged by his sister). The Inner Other becomes the overbearing, constantly present demander who rules from within with an iron hand. The Central I, although usually under the control of the Inner Other, usually finds himself trapped in a place of apparently unresolvable ambiguity as he also has an incontrovertible need to be connected to the life force that is contained within the persona of the instinctual child.

This inner world that we have been exploring from the child's point of view, in this case Bobby's, takes on his own formulation and texture in the individual adult as well. Although the basic characters of the psyche and the principles by which they operate and interact are universal, the way each of us formulates that inner world in symbolic language is as broad and diverse as there are people in the world.

To help understand what this inner world may look like, here is one individual's descriptions of what his world looks like through his mind's eye. This is how this internal arrangement looks in an adult as it was described by the person I called Chris in *Healing the Fractured Self.*

"I can see two parts of me. The one here (his eyes are closed and he holds up his right forearm with the fist clenched) is dark. All I can see are two figures, heads together. They are grotesque, like ceremonial masks. Their teeth are bared. The heads are dark. The other part is on the other side. (He moves his left forearm and fist facing the other fist). It is facing them off. They're at a stalemate. The left side is like the little boy in me. Both of these figures are outside of me. I can feel the struggle outside of me now. It's like it's out there in my arms . . . . And I'm sitting here watching this going on. But watching this, that is the real center of me. It is me. It's like what happened in group a couple of sessions ago. Now I can see what was happening. That part of me (indicating his left arm), the little boy . . . was sitting in my lap, defying everyone, no matter what they said."

The masks are Chris' images of the Inner Others. As he describes them, it is apparent that he has a very clear picture of what he is seeing inside his psychic space. Chris views two figures that appear like "ceremonial" masks with teeth bared. Opposing them is the Little Boy. The mental image, however, is not a static one. Although there is not any "physical" movement in the picture, the Little Boy is in a stand-off with them. A stand-off, as he describes it, that is filled with intense energy.

As he describes this inner activity, who he is as Central I also becomes clear. Both the antagonistic figures stand "outside" him. He is an onlooker in the battle between the two Demons and the Child, his life-giving force. The demons rob him of life. In opposition to them, his Inner Child (his "Turkey") opposes that takeover with stubborn resistance. As they carry on their internal power struggle, they yank him in one direction and then another. But he, as Central I, is ultimately the part of the Self that will choose to listen to one camp over the other.

HANGING ON

Once an internalized image is established, an intense psychic relationship is established with that personal, internalized object. Therefore, even though a child may experience a loss of a parent in the real world, the child is able to maintain a relationship with its internalized parental image. This can be done in either of two ways.

The first is to act out that which the parent approves and then to play out, in the words of the parent, the resulting approval. For example, a child has been told not to take the pots and pans out of a particular kitchen cabinet. She disobeys this rule, and she is scolded and spanked. Afterwards, she goes to her doll house, puts everything inside in order, then plays out the parental approval by saying to a doll, "What a good girl you are for taking care of the house so well."

Not only does the child vicariously regain some of the approval, she also keeps the personal object relationship very much alive through the imaging. In so doing, she keeps the stimulation of the interpersonal event alive and her sense of Self-awareness as well.

The second method is for the child to play out a disobedient scenario in the same way. This time, the doll house is left in shambles. The parental voice is not of approval, but of disapproval. "You naughty girl! Shame on you for leaving the house that way!" Although the internalized relationship has a decidedly negative flavor, it is a relationship, and a very intense one at that—with an intense emotional and psychological connection with the important other residing in and through the guilt, shame, anger and hurt of the event. In this way the parental presence is very much there for the child, even though it is a negative one.

This was the means by which Dana (in chapter six) kept alive her tenuous relationships with her outside parental figures: mother, great aunt and father. Although these internalized figures continued to impose restrictions on her need for Self-expression, she clung to these images in order to preserve her need for interpersonal contact and stimulation which, in turn, fed her sense of Self-awareness and IAM-ness.

But, as we saw earlier, these internalized images really robbed her of her Self-identity. She believed that they were the source of her life and identity. Because of that misbelief, she nurtured them inside her Self and gave more and more of her personal power over to them. The more she did that, the more she needed them, so that by the time she reached chronological adulthood, the internalized others were extremely powerful and Dana's identity was derived mainly from them. As a result of that, however, Dana's own identity was cloudy to her Self and to those around her. This Self-doubt and confusion became increasingly apparent to her and to others as this internal system crystallized inside her.

Thus, the child may come to believe, as Dana did, that she is radically dependent on the power of the parent to survive. Because she fears that any assertion of her autonomy and Self-identity will result in the parent's disfavor and ultimate abandonment, and because the anticipation of that event is so life-threatening, she rarely takes that step on her own.

This, then, becomes the inner system and power arrangement within the psyche of the adult individual who has not successfully worked through that developmental problem:

- The Internal Other remains the central energy of the person, not the "I."
- The "I," as a result, experiences its Self as cut into parts, that is: disintegrated.

With that as an individual's state of mind, his or her possession by the demonic persona is complete. But is this not true of all of us to some extent?

∞9∞

The Demonic Temptation: How the Inner Other Works

THE LAW IN THE LATTER DAYS

One might think that as we grow and progress into later childhood, then adolescence and finally adulthood, these personae created within the psyche would cease to exist. Quite to the contrary, they remain very much alive. In fact, as we get older, these inner characters often grow in power and influence in our daily lives. They are submerged in the unconscious only to manifest themselves, to our consternation and confusion, when we find our Selves in a situation that carries with it a symbolic memory of the old childhood conflicts.

For some of us, these conflicts are not terribly disturbing or troublesome. That's because we experienced our relationship with our parent(s) as, in the main, benign and loving, and our childhood as without trauma. For others, though, whose childhood may have been ridden with ignorance, misguided conceptions about healthy child care, traumas such as death or divorce, or parents who were, at best, not very loving, and at worst, vicious and sadistic, these conflicts continually emerge and rule our lives.

To cope with the negative environment in which he finds his Self, this child constructs Inner Others to manage the trauma or the impact of the dysfunctional parent. However, it is the nature of this kind of Inner Other to label the child as "bad" for having "caused" the trauma or dysfunctional environment. This accusation continues to rule from within throughout the person's life with unrestrained tyranny, keeping the Self its prisoner and slave.

THE CONFLICT

Why then, do we allow the Inner Other to rule us so? The answer appears in the essential conflict we experience as children. Our important others *are* extremely important to our existence—physically and psychologically. The loss of an important other—and therefore the loss of love and connection with that important other—is experienced as a kind of death of the Self by the child.

To conform to the wishes of the important other means, on the one hand, that the child maintains his present sense of identity through the important other; on the other hand, it means the loss, in some degree, of the sense of his identity as separate from the important other. The dilemma for the child becomes, "If I choose to be in a relationship with someone else, I must give up some important part of my Self."

With that as the premise, the child has one of two options: to give up his developing personal, autonomous sense of identity in order to be in a relationship, or to preserve his personal, autonomous sense of identity by giving up his sense of connectedness with the important other. The child therefore finds himself in a position in which he must juggle both these needs.

As we saw in the previous chapters, the child, beginning about the age of eighteen months, becomes increasingly capable of creating an internal image of the important other who accepts and praises certain forms of behavior, and rejects and punishes others. This ability to create internal images reaches its peak between the ages of four and five. These images help the child strike a balance between what others expect of him and the latitude he can allow himself in the discovery of his own autonomous, intrinsic identity.

In the child's mind's eye, however, the internalized imaging of the others is established with the same hierarchy of power that exists between him and his external important others. Just as the external important others are infinitely more important and powerful than the child, the Inner Other is more important and powerful than the child's developing identity as Self.

THE TWO CHOICES

Emanating out of that internal system we create during childhood is a view of the world that determines how we relate to our Selves and to others. The law of life is presented to us by the Inner Other as, "If you want to be in relationship to an other, you must give up yourself, disappear and become what the other wants you to be. If you don't, you will be rejected by the other."

The whole system is based upon other people validating the worth of our being. The specter of being rejected by someone is like a dagger that drives itself into the heart of that old childhood wound. To stop the wound from being reopened into a bloody sore, most of us have devised a system based on one of two possible responses to the internal law dictated to us by our Inner Other.

One response is: "I disconnect myself from the rest of humanity so I can preserve my identity." The "reasoning" behind that choice is, "If I don't connect, I can't be rejected and I won't have to feel the pain of being rejected." The second response is: "I capitulate my identity to the others, I become whatever they want me to be, so that they will not reject me." That is the fundamental starting point of the dialogue that exists between our Selves and the Inner Other voices. It is the base of the temptation by the demonic force or the Inner Other within each of us.

I Am if You Love Me

As an example of the second response, we can look at Dana, whom we met earlier. Her response to this temptation was to believe that she did not possess any significance and substance of her own. She fully believed the Tempter's assertion that her only hope lay in becoming and doing what it predicted others wanted her to do and be. It promised her that, if she followed its prescriptions, others would approve of and like her, validating her value and substance as a person.

However, as she lived out this order of things to its fullest ramifications, she paid a terrible price. This was most evident in a session between Dana and myself recounted in part here:

DANA: Why do I say "you?" . . . You see I don't want to say "I." I want it in the category of everybody so that I'm not . . . it's not happening to me . . . Well, it's a denial in a certain way . . .

I think it doesn't make me feel so alone if I say "you." Then other people experience it . . . There are other people that are . . . that feel this way at times; it's just not . . . it's just not "you" . . .

Sometimes . . . I forget what we've discussed here. Then I listen to a tape, and what I've said comes back to me. . . . I can hear my own voice—how it is at times when I don't feel well, which is most of the time—real dreary. . . . It's like another person. . . . *You* don't recognize *your* own voice. *You* think it's another person. I

> don't know . . . I don't recognize me and other people
> have said that they don't recognize me either . . . I do
> seem like somebody else.

Even as she spoke, she referred to her Self as a "you," as though she was other than her Self. She was evaporating psychologically and spiritually right in front of me. The disintegration of her Self was evident in the confusion and hesitancy of what she was saying. But as she wrestled with the question she was demonstrating well what her internal conflict was.

Once she had given her Self over to her Inner Demons, she believed what they said to her: "You can know nothing about your Self. You are totally incompetent to judge anything about reality, whether it be about your Self or others. Only others can tell you what is real." Having given her Self over to that belief system, she gave up any claim to her own experience. This meant that she had to disclaim her perceptions, feelings, thoughts, needs or wants. Instead she relied on what the others told her about reality (or what she thought they told her). Further, instead of claiming anything for her Self, the only thing she could allow was what she thought the other person might need or want.

GIVING UP STIMULATION STATES

In chapter five, I spoke of the function of the stimulation states. There, we explored how, through the stimulation states, Self-awareness comes alive and unfolds. It is through the stimulation states of feeling, thinking, etc., that each of us becomes aware: I AM WHO I AM.

But because of the activity of her demons, Dana gave up those stimulation states by disowning her perceptions, feelings, thoughts, understandings, judgments, needs and wants. With the stimulation states blunted, her Self-awareness, her YHWH-ness or sense of I WHO AM-ness was radically diminished. The result was that she experienced her Self as an empty core.

The demon had tricked her into this experience of her Self. She so totally believed it to be the truth, she followed the demon's dictates even more assiduously as a way to fill up the terrible internal void she experienced her Self to be. The more she listened to it, the more she felt hollow and empty. And so the downward spiral went.

The more she gave up the stimulation from her experiences as an identified, defined, autonomous, substantial human being, the more necessary it was to hang onto the stimulation she gained from her "connectedness" with others. Because of the dictates of her demons, Dana could not find her sense of IAM-ness. The only place she could turn was to others. The result was that the focus of her existence was on the feelings, thoughts, perceptions, wants and needs of others. Thus, her sense of Self could only come indirectly through the experience of others, but never directly from her Self.

However, what appeared to her to be connectedness with others was really a connectedness with her Inner Demons. What she thought other people wanted from her and wanted her to be were constructions of her demonic voices. It was the demons who said to her, "If you do it this way; If you feel this; If you don't feel that; If you don't think that; If you do this for them . . . then they will like you." The other person Dana thought she was pleasing was really a mirage, constructed by the Demonic Power within her. So, not even her connectedness with the other person was real. The only connectedness—and the only source of stimulation that could confirm her sense of IAM-ness—was not her Self, or even another person. It was her powerful and intense relationship with her demonic persona.

So complete was her dissolution of her Self, that even as we talked, she lost her Self. She was so disconnected, so nonpresent to her Self that she couldn't remember anything we talked about. Even as she was struggling to be within her Self in the examination of her behavior, she slipped out of her Self again when she said, "It's like another person. You don't recognize your own voice. You think it's another person." And, as she was slipping outside of her Self again, the impact made itself felt when she then said, "I don't recognize me . . . I do seem like somebody else." That sums it up! She is somebody else. Not being able to be her Self, she became a nobody, a non-person.

GIVING UP CONNECTIONS

Chris, another person I examined in *Healing the Fractured Self*, took the other fork in the path offered by the demonic presence. Instead of giving up his identity to others as a way of surviving, he held on to his identity for dear life. In so doing, he thought it was necessary to forsake any connection with others. Unlike Dana, he did not disown his perceptions, feelings, needs, wants and desires . . . as long as he was alone.

That was the problem with his system—he had to be alone in the world in order to make it work. True, while he was alone, he knew who he was in his feelings, wants and desires. He was able to compensate for the lack of stimulation of interpersonal contact by investing in activities that stimulated him from within—like reading, drawing, thinking, reflecting, walking, watching the world around him without getting involved in it. Because this was his fundamental life choice he became an isolated, personal capsule floating in an impersonal sea of others.

BALANCING THE DIET

Our stimulation diet is very much like our food diet: if we don't vary and balance the diet, we'll become diseased or ill. When we don't balance our stimulation diet, we experience feelings that warn us that we're not getting the variety we need to maintain the proper level of the IAM Self-aware state. Loneliness is such a feeling.

It seems that the need for social interaction is an intrinsic aspect to our human makeup. It's very clear from all the archaeological evidence we have that we (as well as the primates in general) are highly social. As our ability to be Self-aware evolved, the need for interpersonal stimulation became a part of the package by which IAM-ness manifested itself. Loneliness warns the human organism that this form of stimulation is sufficiently absent to compromise its ability to maintain Self-awareness.

This was the chronic state in which Chris found his Self. He feared the loss of identity he would experience if he allowed his Self to be in relationship with others, so he cut his Self off from that very necessary source of stimulation. It's as if he attempted to live entirely on a diet of carbohydrates without any intake of protein. Although he might be consuming adequate quantities of calories, without protein his cells could not maintain growth and energy. Without the stimulation that comes from significant bonds with others, he was spiritually starving his Self to death.

Like the person who would eat only carbohydrates, he did not regard his Self as starving. Loneliness was a feeling he found difficult to understand and admit. If he did, he would have to challenge his choice to "go it alone." So the unrecognized and unacknowledged loneliness created an inner restlessness and sense of void. This coincided with his experience of his Self and what his Inner Demon said about him, "See, you are nothing—nothing but garbage!" Hearing that, he would retreat even more into his shell, which then caused the loneliness to increase in intensity. The restlessness and the resultant inner attack would likewise increase. The downward spiral would become increasingly intense with the completion of each cycle.

THE TEMPTATIONS IN THE DESERT AND IN THE PSYCHE

Dana and Chris are real people whose inner conflicts represent the conflicts we all have. The universality of these conflicts and the activities of the Inner Demons led me to one of the earliest theological insights I had by connecting these inner psychological processes with Jesus' mission among us.

A number of years ago, I found myself confronted with the task of preparing a homily that was to be based on the temptations of Jesus in the desert as related in Matt. 4:1–11 and discussed here in chapter six.

One day I was showering when disconnected thoughts about this story washed over me like the hot water that coursed over my head and body. Suddenly a question arose in me: "Aren't the three temptations offered to Jesus by Satan really the same temptations that pull at Chris and Dana?" I jumped out of the shower, hurriedly dried myself, and ran to get a pen and pad to write down the thoughts and realizations as they flooded in on me. The story began to shine with a new light.

The First Temptation: Going It Alone

I realized almost immediately that the first temptation—the taunt by the Devil to change stones into bread—was a trick by the demon to seduce us to go it alone. "If you have bread," says the demon, "you have everything you need. You don't need anyone else. If you don't need anyone else, you don't have to give up your Self by being in a relationship." This, of course, was the temptation into which Chris most often fell: it was the major spiritual choice of his life pattern.

How did Chris come to make this choice? His mother was a very angry woman who vented her rage at anyone who happened to be standing nearby, whether it was her husband or one of her children. Chris learned early that it was dangerous for him to be who he was in her presence. It was a necessary act of survival to hide his Self from this sadistic woman.

From his earliest days he listened to epithets from his mother like, "You're nothing but garbage." These were hurled not only at him, but also at his brothers (all of whom spent most of their adult years in and out of prisons) and before them, their father. In a very real sense, then, Chris lived in a psychological environment of disregard for the sanctity of his being and the being of others by his mother, his most important other. In order to protect his Self from the pain of that cruel reality, he took that maternal voice inside his psyche as a way of warning him that he was getting too close to precipitating an attack. That voice became his demon, the internalized image of his mother.

Because he was so vulnerable to these degradations of his Self, a part of him took that voice very seriously. This part of him became the child allied with the Inner Other. This Inner Child came to some conclusions which continued to live inside Chris, affecting him as an adult in a very active and powerful way.

The first conclusion was that his Inner-Mother-Demon was correct about his inner emptiness and valuelessness. The second conclusion was that the world of others was a dangerous, unfriendly and alien place, which brought only the pain of rejection and abandonment. The child inside him said, "If we don't hide, everyone will find out that we really are nothing more than a heap of smelly garbage. We'd better stay hidden from view."

In response to the real experience of his vicious and sadistic mother, this part of his Self realized, "I'd better not show her my pain. If she sees it, she will use that against me also. So I'll stay inside my Self and, that way, she can't hurt me."

Chris set his Self up to be an ally with the very person he was legitimately and realistically able to define as his enemy. At the time, this wasn't a bad rule. It was dangerous to let his mother get close. However, as Chris grew up, he thought everyone was like his mother, and he defined the rest of the world in the same way. As a result, he applied this rule to all other persons. Chris also feared he would experience personal rejection and abandonment by others if they discovered his "garbageness." So he kept others at arm's length. With these two powerful reasons as the motivation for keeping his Self isolated from others, he in fact became the ally of his Mother-Demon. But in so doing, he became a slave to it as well.

He came to believe that he had to live by bread alone. He relinquished his need and right to have close and loving relationships with others. As a result, his loneliness generated a deep sense of inner emptiness that ate at his soul. His experience of his IAM-ness became badly tarnished. The cruel irony of all this is that he ended up living in a very close, intense relationship with the very persona from whom he originally fled in justifiable fear.

Dana fell into the same trap. There would be times when the clouds of guilt, worthlessness and Self-doubt would leave and Dana would achieve a temporary strength and aliveness. At those times she would move from an entwined dependency on her husband (in which she would plead with him to stay in bed with her, not go to work, or ask him for advice on making the smallest decisions) to a position of cool, aloof independence from him. She would communicate with him only on a very superficial level, would move away from his touches, and would generally not want to be around him very much.

During those times, she perceived closeness with another as a sign of weakness and dependency; an inability to function on her own. When Dana was a child, the only time she got any attention was when she was ill. At those times, her mother would dote on her, giving her special food and spending time with her (which never happened when she was well). Out of that primal experience she came to construct a Mother-Demon who said to her, "If you are to be loved, you must be sick. When you are sick, go to bed and stay there, and I'll love you by taking care of your every need. When you are well, you are not lovable and therefore don't deserve my love." A part of Dana remained that little girl who thought that she had to be radically dependent on, and vulnerable to the other if she was to be loved.

When she capitulated to this inner system, it brought on the excruciatingly painful loss of identity. Because of its intensity, she would flee from anything she thought might cause such pain. Therefore, she fled intimacy.

Chris and Dana, however, (along with the rest of us) were created to be in relationship for, as it is related in the Genesis story (2:18): "Then the Lord said, 'It is not good for a person to be alone so I will create someone who can be a companion and helper.'" Our modern day Adam and Eve (Chris and Dana) were blocked from that life-giving warmth of intimacy. They came to believe, because of the activity of Inner Demons, that closeness with others meant the death of the Self. The irony is that it was the demons who brought death by not allowing them to be free to find others who would be willing to love and respect them for who they are.

The Second Temptation: If You Love Me, You Will Rescue Me

When the first temptation in the desert fails, Satan takes Jesus to the pinnacle of the temple and says, "If you are truly the Son of God, throw yourself down! For isn't it written that 'God will have his angels watch over you and bear you up lest you strike your foot against a stone'?" To that taunt Jesus replied, "It is also written that you will not tempt the Lord your God." The second temptation appeals to the belief that love is defined by one person's willingness to let another take over the responsibility for his Self. "If you are the Son of God, throw your Self down and God will save you," says Satan. In other words, "Defy the natural laws of gravity, consider your Self exempt from them, because if God really loves you, God will take over the responsibility for your actions." Whether we're talking about God taking over the responsibility for our lives in our actions, thoughts, feelings, or desires, or whether we expect the same of our spouse, lover, friend, parent, child—whomever—we expect *someone* to take over for us. This is the nature of the second temptation.

This became very clear one day in a session in which Dana and her husband Bob had just come from an appointment with the doctor. It was a Monday and Dana had been having abdominal pains all weekend. Throughout the entire weekend she kept begging Bob to tell her what medication to take. Then, when he did take over this responsibility, she resented him because he was telling her what to do!

That morning, they went to the doctor. At the doctor's office, Dana again became very angry with Bob because he was asking all the questions. When I asked her what she was angry about, she said, "I thought he was treating me like a child." When I asked Bob why he behaved that way, he said that whenever they went to the doctor, Dana would not ask questions. Then she would come home and pester him for the answers. By asking Bob to make the medical decisions for her, she was capitulating to the second temptation: "To show me you are lovable, give yourself over to the Other. If they rescue you, that will prove you are lovable because you are worth enough to be rescued." When Dana wanted her husband to tell her what she was feeling, perceiving, needing, wanting, she had fallen victim to the second temptation.

There were times when Chris expected members of his therapy group to "know" that he was in pain without his telling anyone. At those times, he also succumbed to the temptation. When we are asked by someone, "What would you like to do this evening?" and our response is, "Oh, I don't know. What would you like to do?" we too are being tempted. We are attempting to dodge the responsibility for our own needs, and trying to seduce the other person into defining us according to their needs.

Contained within the second temptation is a certain understanding of love. On the one hand, it dictates, "If God loves you, He will take over for you." On the other hand, it also implies, "If you love God, you will let God take over for you." To put it in purely human terms, "If a person loves you, the person will take over for you by guessing what you need, and making your decisions for you." By extension, this also means, "If you love the other person, you will let the person take you over." This is the way both Chris and Dana defined love.

The Third Temptation: If You Worship Me, I Will Give You Power over Others

In the final temptation the demon takes Jesus to a high mountain and says, "I will give you power over all these kingdoms and principalities if you fall down and worship me." What are these kingdoms and principalities that Satan promises us if we do bow down and worship him?

Dana (and Chris for that matter) was seduced by the demon to believe that it had the power to grant her substance and worth. Along with that would come power and authority over other people's minds and hearts. This all would be given her if she was willing to turn over the ultimate power, authority and responsibility for her existence to the demon. To "fall down and worship" means, "If you follow everything I tell you to do in relationship to others, I have the power to make them love you. I know what is in the minds of all (don't I know what is in your mind?). If you follow everything I tell you, you will be able to do everything everyone wants of you, and you will become what everyone wants. You will have the power to make all people love you; then you will fill that deep void that is within you. And you know how much you need that void to be filled."

Fundamentally, then, Chris's and Dana's demons told them if they followed their advice and predictions, they could hide their underlying worthlessness, badness and guilt. This required that they listen slavishly to everything the demons told them. Any slip-up would result in revealing the "secret" and they would be exposed for what they really were, ugly and misshapen. It's not enough to just listen to the demons, we must worship them by hanging onto every word they might utter into our inner ear.

Essentially, what the demons were saying to Dana and Chris was that they needed to know what others wanted of them before they even spoke it. If they waited for the other person to speak it out loud, they might inadvertently do something "to offend" the other person. This meant they required the power to read people's minds. "I can tell you what others want you to be and what they want of you, if you listen to me," the demons said, "and if you do that, I can guarantee you will not be rejected by anyone. But if you do not, I can also guarantee that you will be rejected and your secret will be known by all. And you know how you will feel then. So you had better listen to me."

Here's a simple example of mind reading: one day, during a session, Dana became aware that I was sitting with my arms crossed and assumed I was angry with her. Her demons had convinced her that mind reading, the ability to "know" why somebody was doing something or what someone else was thinking, was more accurate and real than the other's own testimony. By reading other people's minds, Dana could alter the behavior that "caused" someone to see her in an unfavorable light. She could preserve others' good opinion of her, or sidestep any negative opinion they might have of her. If, at any point, someone did not think well of her (or she thought that was the case), she knew she was to blame. Obviously, she hadn't listened closely enough to the demons. This, then, was a failure to worship the demon.

The penalty for this failure was a terrible sense of guilt, a deeper loss of value manifested in shame and a more profound sense of inner emptiness. Therefore, the power to mind read was clung to with great tenacity because it forestalled all those other negative states of mind.

In actuality, the reason I was sitting that way was because the room was cold and I was trying to keep warm. It made a great impact on Dana to hear the difference between her projection on me and what was actually happening in me.

Another power promised to anyone who worships the demon is the ability to predict the future. An example of this power of futurizing occurred one day when Dana came for her session, visibly upset. When I asked her what was troubling her, she told me that she was going to be unable to keep a shopping date with a new friend that Friday because she had fallen badly behind in her Christmas preparations. When I asked her why she didn't simply call her friend and explain her problem, her response was, "I'm afraid I'll make her angry and she won't want me as a friend."

So solidly was the anticipated response implanted in Dana, this predicted event had become a present reality. She could not call the woman because, in her mind, there could be no other response beyond the one predicted by the demon. I proposed to her that the woman might be just as hassled by the Christmas rush as she was and might, in fact, be relieved to have a rain check. Because Dana did not entertain this possibility; she exclaimed, "Why, I never thought of that!"

Because there was no room for another perspective beyond the demon's predictions, Dana was unable to stand back and test the accuracy of its predictions. By mind reading and futurizing, she was tricked and seduced into believing the demons granted her what they promised. In reality, however, they did not deliver love and relationship. Instead they gave her disconnectedness from her Self and others. This, again, brought about the very spiritual death she was trying so desperately to avoid.

When Dana actually did go to her friend and explain her position, the woman was in fact relieved, because she found her Self in the same time-bind as Dana (as I had suggested). The reality created in Dana's mind did not in fact exist. But because of her intense relationship to her demon, Dana created a mental mirage of her new friend. Because she believed that her demons had the power to predict the future about the woman, Dana had entered into a profound relationship with this mirage.

Being a mirage, it was not real, not actually there. It was a no-thing. Relating to a no-thing, but believing she was in relationship with a some-thing, Dana was tricked and deceived by the demon. In actuality, Dana was in a relationship with her very own demon.

The relationship it promised Dana was not delivered; it delivered a no-thing, itself. Dana, seduced into relating to a mirage, was relating to nothing. Relating to nothing, the stimulation she experienced was a sham that only exacerbated her already impoverished sense of IAM-ness. Instead of the power and life it promised her if she worshiped it, Dana's demon brought her powerlessness and death.

The Devil is clever and cunning. In the third temptation, the Devil makes us think: "If I can't have power and control over my own exis-tence because I am compelled to hand it over to the other (thereby los-ing my sense of substance about my Self), I can fill up that void by becoming responsible for and exercising power and control over the other." We are deluded by the demon into believing the other gives us substance and worth. Through the third temptation, not only does the demon seduce us into believing that it knows what others want us to become, but it also seduces us into believing that it knows how others need us to take over and run their lives!

IN SUMMARY

When the Soul falls victim to the demon, and it promises a world of intimacy, the only thing we get is intimacy with the demon. When we give our Selves over to the tempter-demon, we lose our Selves to it. The more the Soul loses her Self, the more she becomes dependent on the advice and direc-tives of the tempter. The demon becomes increasingly active. More and more, we're convinced we cannot function without the demon's input. The bond between the Self and the tempter becomes ever more solidly cement-ed. Everything must be turned over to the demon. The Self must die.

The tempter leads us into an endless labyrinth of mind reading and futurizing; this in turn creates mirages of those who are around us and they "die" to the Self as well. Because we're mainly in relationship to mirages created by the demonic presence, the only person with whom we're real-ly in relationship is the tempter. This is a sorry plight, when we give all to the demon. It promises to give everything back; what it delivers, howev-er, is a bag of magic tricks that have no more substance than a puff of smoke.

∞10∞

Exorcism

IT IS ENOUGH TO BE HUMAN

The temptation in the desert begins the final redemptive round in the resolution of the original conflict that surrounds our creation. At the outset of our story, we are created in the image and likeness of the IAM-ness of God. However, the temptation and fall in the Garden of Eden brings about the degradation of the beauty of that creation. The fall of humankind (from being God's special reflection to desperate alienation from the benevolent Creator) cries out for resolution. The beginning of that resolution is found in Jesus' responses to the Prince of Darkness.

When we look at his rejoinders to the demonic power in the light of the dynamics we've been exploring as a part of our psychospiritual heritage, Jesus' responses are very different from the way we answer to this same force in our lives. Just as his response to the tempter is different, so too is the outcome of the interaction.

Although the underlying assumption that hounds us, "You are empty and, therefore, not worthy," is not explicitly contained in the temptation story, a closer look reveals it to be there by implication. Twice the tempter says to Jesus, "If you are the Son of God . . ." Contained in that phrase is a taunt: "If you think you are so good, prove it to me." Such a challenge is designed to demonstrate to us how impotent we are in contrast to the power of the tempter-taunter. When we discover our Selves to be incapable of meeting the challenge, we experience an inner powerlessness that is used by the taunter to entrap us into slavery.

This manipulation by the tempter does not touch Jesus, however. Unlike our Selves, Jesus is not sucked into the underlying assumption that tricks us into becoming the demon's slave, which is: "If you believe your Self to be so good, you can and must exercise power over the material world and override the fundamental laws of the world (change stones into bread, defy the laws of gravity). Only if you can demonstrate to me that you have these kinds to powers can you prove that you have enough worth to be the Son of God." In other words, we must prove to the Tempter that we have power over the universe.

This, of course, is the trap into which most of us fall. We come to believe that, through the activity of our demons, we should be able to transcend the physical laws of the universe by being able to read others' minds. We are also supposed to be able to predict the future. We're supposed to know what another wants or needs before he or she wants or needs anything. If we fail to accomplish these kinds of deeds, we show our Selves unworthy of approbation and approval by the demon force.

The demon force has convinced us that its approbation and approval is essential in order for our substance and worth to be validated. The failure to gain its approval means that we have no substance or worth. Once we agree that the demon force has the power to grant us these qualities—as well as the authority to define the criteria by which they are to be granted—we are under its power.

But in order to gain the demon's approval, we have to have a 100 percent success rate at mind reading and futurizing. Anything less means failure. The reality is, of course, that no one can ever read another's mind or predict the future. The best any one can do is to guess well. We can never actualize the absolute perfection the demon requires for us to have "substance and worth." Therefore, within the demon-spawned belief system, enslavement is inevitable.

In the first temptation, Satan assumes that his authority to grant Jesus worth and substantiality will not be questioned or challenged. He therefore expects that Jesus will succumb, as the rest of humanity has, to the temptation. He expects that Jesus will try to prove his worth and substantiality by transcending the laws of the physical universe, that is, by trying to change the stones into bread—and fail.

Satan assumes that Jesus, as a human, has one of two choices: he will either accept the challenge or not. Satan assumes that if Jesus chooses to avoid the challenge, it is because he fears he will lose. And if he makes that choice, he demonstrates that he is weak and, therefore, imperfect, and exposes his emptiness and valuelessness.

His other choice is to accept the demon's challenge. If he does that, he (being human) will most certainly fail, as no one can transcend the physical laws of the universe. Therefore, in the eyes of the demonic power, no matter which of the two choices Jesus may make, he demonstrates his inadequacy and, therefore, his worthlessness. The demon, therefore, anticipates that Jesus will be caught in the same trap as the rest of us.

However, Jesus neatly sidesteps this dilemma because he is able to see the deeper issues. The tempter assumes that Jesus, like all other human persons, has to prove his Self to be superhuman: "Prove to me you are the Son of God by showing you stand outside the physical laws of the universe."

Throughout its history, the human species has been tricked by this lie: that our limitation is the imperfection that renders us worthless. The only way the worthlessness can be abrogated is to demonstrate that we are without limit, super human. The Satan who is attempting to seduce Jesus assumes that he, too, is caught in this dilemma. Either he reveals that fatal flaw or he attempts to hide it by appearing to be more powerful than us.

This premise is contained in each of the three temptations. Each of the three times, though, Jesus is able to say to the demon, "You do not have power and authority over me. There is another who does have authority over me, my Father. To him I do not need to prove anything by doing extraordinary things. It is enough for him that I AM WHO I AM."

It Is Not Good for Humankind to Be Alone

The demon's first overture is constructed in such a way that it appears to offer a way out of this dilemma. It proposes to Jesus that he will not be discovered as imperfect if there is no one to discover it; that is, to stay alone in the world: "Command these stones to become loaves of bread (and you'll have all you need to sustain you. You will not have to depend on another to sustain your Self. You will not have to leave your private space and reveal your Self to anyone, thereby revealing your imperfections and, therefore, your worthlessness)." If Jesus' response is to perform the miracle, he accepts the premise that he needs to prove something to Satan.

The tempter, however, is foiled in its endeavor to seduce Jesus in this way. Jesus refuses to grant the demon any authority over him. Instead, he turns to God's authorship of humankind: "A person shall not live by bread alone, but by every word that proceeds from the mouth of God." But what is the word to which Jesus is referring?

In the opening of Genesis 1, it is said by God that humankind is created in God's image and likeness. Adam's and Eve's, Dana's and Chris's, man's and woman's essential character is that of IAM-ness, to be in the imaged likeness in God. Within that IAM-ness is substance and worth that needs no act nor anyone else to substantiate that it is!

We are truly the children, the progeny of God. Because of that, we have a profoundly intimate connection with our Heavenly Parent. In that context, humankind is given the world as a gift from God: "Behold, (because you are good) I have given you every plant yielding seed which is upon the face of all the earth and every tree . . ." (Gen. 1:29).

Not only has God given humankind the world as Her gift, but God breathes into Adam's nostrils the very breath of life (Gen. 2:7). How much more intimate can a relationship be? We are created full beings of substance who can receive the breath of God and breathe it as well. In Jesus' response to Satan, he is reiterating this fundamental premise of our existence. By answering the tempter at this level, its taunts are deflated and the fall of the power of darkness over us is being orchestrated by Jesus.

Further, God does not create Adam to be in intimacy only with his Self. To make sure that Adam will not be lonely for his own kind, Eve is created to be a helper and a partner; they complete each other's being. So while Adam slept, God took one of his ribs and woman was created (Gen. 2:18, 21, 22). Not only are man and woman, Adam and Eve, to be companions in life with each other; they are also meant to be companions in intimacy with each other.

Thus, when the Inner Demon of Darkness tempts anyone to go it alone, it violates our fundamental human dignity, which is to include connection and intimacy with others. Jesus' response to the tempter reestablishes that dignity, affirms our fundamental human worth, and attests to the powerlessness of the demon. Jesus proclaims again our preordained destiny to live life in the fullness of worth and substance, in intimacy with others, both human and divine.

You Are Empowered to Run Your Life

In the second temptation, Satan is trying to seduce Jesus into manipulating another (God) into taking responsibility for his life. Now, this is exactly the temptation Dana succumbed to when she hounded her husband to tell her what medication to take. The assumption is: "If I do anything for my Self, I will not be able to do it 'right' and I will be condemned for being 'imperfect.' Imperfection means I am no good, so I must avoid that at all costs. If I can turn responsibility for my Self over to another, I cannot be accused of doing anything 'wrong.' And that other person who takes over for me, demonstrates that they really love me because they shield me from the pain that I would otherwise feel if my imperfection were revealed to the world."

Jesus, however, responds in a very different way to this temptation by saying, "A person should not tempt the Lord God." This response deflates the temptation in several ways.

One of our essential human qualities is the awareness of our identity or IAM-ness. When Dana gave up the power over and responsibility for her Self, that sense of identified IAM-ness evaporated. God created her to be the unique manifestation of His Being through her being. But, when she gave up responsibility for her Self, that uniqueness in God's image and likeness was lost. Thus, God's creative design for her was lost. This loss was a sacrilege, an offense against the intent and creative act of God.

In God's creative act, powers are given to each human being adequate for that person. Furthermore, God gave each of us the free will to exercise these powers or to choose not to. We are meant to draw from our inner resources and not to turn to anyone else to override them—not even God. In other words, God also wanted us to be autonomous from Him. That autonomy is intrinsic to our human nature.

Capitulating our autonomy to anyone, human or divine, interrupts qualities of the human soul that God meant to be intrinsic. Jesus' response to Satan claims fully God's creative gift to humankind: "It is sufficient for me to be who I am without adding the power of another (even God). I do not need another to assume responsibility for me. To expect that would defile what God has already given me. Further, I do not have anything to prove to you, Satan. For anything you would grant me is already contained within me." Jesus quite clearly says that to give up responsibility for and power over one's existence is sacrilege.

THE THIRD TEMPTATION

The demon preys on humanity by keeping alive our childhood belief that we do not have enough inner resources to cope with the tasks and events of life, and are therefore imperfect. It has further convinced us that, if others should find us out, they will considered us worthless. In the system of the demon, if we are considered to be worthless by others, we *are* worthless. So, as long as we are within this system it is extremely important for us to hide our imperfection.

And that is exactly what we do. We enter into a system of secrets that binds us to Satan with chains. It is this system of secret-keeping that constitutes the power of the third temptation ("worship me and I will give you all").

In the Satanic system, any mistake, no matter how large or small, is a terrible, unforgivable sin. This is what forces us to avoid claiming any decision or act for our Selves. Furthermore, this requires that we turn over responsibility for any decision or act to someone else. In the third temptation, the demon promises that if we listen to it, we will not have to worry about making mistakes. Thus, the "person" we should trust to take over for us, who will make the "perfect" decision, is the demon.

However, as we found out through what happened to Dana, when we succumb to that seduction, it generates a profound experience of inner void. To fill up that emptiness, we assume the demon into that void, which gives us some sense—albeit false—of inner substance. By capitulating to the demon in this temptation, it appears as though we gain a great deal. The reality is, though, that it engulfs and eviscerates our souls.

THE GOD EXORCISM

Unlike our Selves, Jesus' response to that final temptation is immediate, emphatic, and definitive. "Get out of here, Satan! A person shall worship and serve only the Lord God." As a result, Jesus does not succumb to this temptation.

Jesus is able to turn to Satan, the monarch of darkness, and cast it out emphatically, without dispute: "You cannot grant me power over others, for it is not yours to grant. Even God in all His glory will not exercise that kind of power over his beloved children! Get out of here!" With that the demon slinks away.

In his responses to the temptations, Jesus rekindles the possibility of freedom from the enslavement of the tempter. The freedom he brings to us though, is not one in which he magically frees us once and for all from the demon's power. Rather, he begins the process by giving witness to our intrinsic goodness and worth. He then models for us a new way of engaging Satan—which makes us, as humans, the victors.

OUR PERSONAL EXORCISM

In order for Chris and Dana to end their bombardment by their demons, they would have to move from their old responses to the demons to ones similar to those of Jesus. It is Jesus' model I rely on as I assist others in freeing their Selves from their slavery to the Prince of Darkness.

Another person, whom I shall call Abel, had an engagement with his demon during a session that encapsulates the temptation, how he initially fell prey to the wiles of his demons, how he turned himself around by acknowledging the temptation, his confrontation of the demons with his IAM-ness, and his eventual victory over them.

The precipitating issue for Abel was his indecisiveness about his commitment to marry the woman with whom he had been involved for several years. We talked many times about the very positive, reinforcing, connected relationship he had with this woman. Yet, this awareness seemed to repeatedly get lost and quickly evaporate.

At one point in our conversation, he referred to the mental dialogue in which he found himself engaged when he mulled over whether he would or would not marry Susan. I suggested it might be helpful if he could speak that familiar internal dialogue out loud so we could both hear it:

ABEL: Well, I'll be thinking about my love for Susan and the dialogue goes something like this: (Abel here speaks out loud the dialogue between himself and the demon in his psyche). Yes, I really love her.

DEMON: You don't have enough feeling for her to say that you love her.

ABEL: But I do have a sense of peace, of fulfillment, of trust when I'm with her.

DEMON: But you don't have enough. You're not committed enough.

ABEL: What's enough?

DEMON: You don't have the euphoria that you should be experiencing if you were really in love.

ABEL: But I'm thirty-eight years old and the feelings that I have for her are the kinds of feelings that would make a good marriage and a father of children.

DEMON: You can't adjust to living with one person at an intense level, plus having kids kicking at you, demanding that you get up in the middle of the night.

ABEL: I think I can adjust to that at the time it happens.

DEMON: No, it's too painful to you.

ABEL: I don't care about the pain. I don't want to be alone.

DEMON: Yes you do want to be alone, because you can survive that way without pain.

ABEL: But the pain is the loneliness.

DEMON: You are different from other people. You can't adjust to a lot of changes. You can't. You can't. I tell you, you can't.

ABEL: I believe I can and I want to try. And with Susan, I have a supporting person who can help me. I want Susan.

DEMON: OK, but you'll be sorry.

THE DYNAMICS OF THE INTERNAL CONVERSATION

The first observation we can make in response to Abel's internal conversation is that it is clearly an I-You interchange. This suggests that there is some internal "being" who stands outside Abel's IAM, his being, but within his psyche who speaks to him, and to whom Abel responds as he would to any one of us.

As Abel and his adversary engage in confrontation, the presumptions of the tempter sound very much like those of Satan in his exchange with Jesus. The difference here is that Abel's adversary taunts and tricks him, not letting a chance go by to put him down, to castrate him, to rob him of power, to denigrate his feelings, needs, wants and ability to cope.

I suggested that he listen to the tape of the internal dialogue he had just spoken out loud. When he finished, he commented: "It's relentless! The voice just keeps taking everything I say and dumping more shit back onto me. There was a lot of the use of 'but.' I say one thing—'but— you're not looking at the total picture.' And he denigrates the feelings I do have. They're dismissed as being inauthentic or insignificant or irrelevant!

"I know there is a deception going on because the question keeps coming to me about the lack of feeling. I sit down and write things about Susan and I make a list a mile long about my feelings. So I know that it's a crock of shit that I'm not feeling anything. I'm feeling all kinds of things. He's just trying to play a game with me, especially when he says 'No, you can't do it.' By God, I'm going to get him. (Laugh) I'm going to get him!"

Up to this point, Abel had been losing the battle with his demon voice because he has agreed to argue with it. At this point I suggest to Abel that we listen to the tape again. This time, however, I suggested that he reconsider his responses to the demon. Rather than respond in argument, I suggested he be confrontative.

A NEW RESPONSE

As Abel listened to the first interchange, he recognized again how profoundly the demon discounted his feelings for Susan. He also began to realize the violation he had been suffering at the hands of this internal demon. His anger about this began to well up, and words and sentences began to flow as well. At this point I brought out a five-foot stuffed dummy bag onto which Abel could direct his remarks—and punches. "I have my feelings and they are my feelings. How dare you say, 'Not enough!' They're ME. They are MY feelings. You can't tell me what's enough and what's not enough. Who are you comparing me to? Well, I'm not going to be compared anymore!"

As we continued listening to the tape, Abel became increasingly aware of an entire list of issues to which he capitulates as he argues with the demon. No matter what he might do or say, in the eyes of the demon, it is never enough. Furthermore, any action Abel might want to take in the future, like getting married and having kids, is immediately discounted by this inner darkness as totally out of the realm of Abel's capability. The demon always has an answer that undermines any positive feeling Abel might have for his Self. In other words, it is always ready with some kind of put-down to keep Abel in its orbit of power. As a result, Abel is always in a position of belittlement in relation to this inner voice. Arguing with the demon, Abel finds himself being drawn into a very tight circle in which the demon holds the power. At one point he realizes, "I'm trying to prove or refute. I think I'm doing it because I feel insecure about what it's saying and I've got to prove it to my Self. But the argument is not with me, it's with him."

Realizing this, Abel responded: "I don't have to convince you. You're nothing! (hits) You're garbage (hits) in my life. I'm going to get you out of there (hits) so I don't talk to you and don't deal in your categories. (hits) I've got to listen to my little boy inside. I don't have to prove my existence to you, you bastard! (hits) I AM! I'm not going to listen to your bullshit anymore! You're a temptation to me! I think that if I can convince you and answer all your arguments, I'll (hits) be OK. Well, your arguments are garbage. (hits) I only have to BE and not listen to you (hits)."

THE EFFECTS OF EXORCISM

As a result of this confrontation with the demon (which went on for quite a while), Abel successfully exorcised his Self of its presence and activity. A month later, he asked Susan to marry him. Six months later, they were married and were leading a happy, successful life together. They were both aware of their Inner Other voices. They helped each other listen for them and confront them when they occurred. When the demon tried to return to undermine his relationship with Susan, Abel reminded himself and it of this confrontation, and the temptation was deflated. Because Abel and Susan have committed themselves to avoid mind reading and futurizing, their relationship continued to grow into a positive bond with each other. Both admitted, however, that it calls for constant vigilance against the voice of darkness.

I chose the name of Abel for this man because one of his inner voices was the voice of his jealous older brother. Abel frequently recalled bickering with his brother as a young child, as siblings do. Whenever Abel experienced his Self winning an argument, his brother would have the last word by saying, "Oh well, you're just adopted anyway." The argument would end with his brother as the uncontested victor. This statement had the same effect as the demon saying, "OK you'll be sorry." Because of the devastation he experienced as a child, a kind of emotional murder occurred when Abel tried to claim and live out his adult life as a responsible, feeling, loving person. The knowledge that there was an Inner-Brother-Demon, and that he could respond differently to that Brother-Demon—not as a helpless, gullible weak sibling, but as an adult —freed him from that ancient enslavement.

Like Abel, Chris (Adam) and Dana (Eve) fought their winning battles with their demons. Each battle won brought them closer to the final victory over the inner despots. This is what each of us must do.

THE NEW LAW

When Jesus responded to Satan the way he did, he proposed a new law by which to consider the Self-in-the-world-of-others than that which was presented by the Prince of Darkness. Essentially, when Abel confronted his demons, he followed that new law:

1. I am the only person who knows what is going on inside of my Self, and you are the only one who knows what is going on inside of your Self.
2. I have the responsibility to articulate that to my Self and to you; but you have the responsibility to articulate to your Self and the rest of the world your internal experience of your Self.
3. I have power, authority and responsibility over my existence; you have power, authority and responsibility over yours.

When we meet and interact, the contract of that interaction is one in which we mutually state who we are from our own respective centers. We accept responsibility for something that is within our own grasp, that is reasonable, and is our right and responsibility: handling our Selves. If we can't, no one else can.

If this is the base from which two or more people agree to relate, then the old neurotic equation becomes a new order of Self-health: I am responsible for my Self (=) you are responsible for your Self. I need not be preoccupied with preserving my Self from disappearing into the other. With "I AM" as the starting point, I am guaranteed to remain whole in my IAM-ness.

THE WEANING

Early in life, Chris and Dana unknowingly chose to ally their Selves with the Inner Demon. Their lives then operated according to the rules established by the demonic personae within them. The most fundamental rule they were constrained to follow did not allow them to make any decision, think any thought, or feel any feeling that was not dictated by these inner tyrants.

With Jesus' new law as the operating principle, however, we don't violate our Selves. We affirm our Selves as we draw from the experience of our Selves, and as we relate to others. We don't violate others; with our Selves as the base we see others as they really are. We don't accept the mirages to which the demon would have us relate. We allow others to speak for their Selves. We hear each other, and can weigh all the information we have about each other. We listen to what is being said without the contamination of our own assumptions. Once we have done that, we can respond to each other, within the limitations of who each one of us is at that moment in time.

The Inner Demon not only robbed Chris and Dana of substance, but it also deprived them of relationship with others in which they could rest in peaceful harmony. The world of others appeared to be a hostile one in which they were either ignored or attacked by others. Chris and Dana were beginning to discover, however, that if they were able to exercise their Selves over these evil spirits who dwelled within them, the sense of peace and tranquility they yearned after could be theirs.

With this as the operating principle, the demon has no room to operate. Jesus showed us a way by which we can dethrone the Inner Power of Darkness. He presented a model by which we might be freed from its power. As the Incarnation of the Godhead, he reestablished for us our original inheritance—the inherent goodness and substance of our IAM-ness. In so doing, God blessed us again.

PART III

Jesus and Our Inner Children

∞11∞

<u>Unless You Become As Little Children</u>

THE UNCLEAN SPIRIT

The process Abel went through in the confrontation and casting out of his Inner Other Demon was certainly very healing for him. Together, he and I had cast out the unclean spirit once, twice, many times. There was the initial sense of freedom, relief and release that came with the exorcism. I found out, however, as did Abel and other clients with whom I had worked throughout the years, that we couldn't leave the inner healing process there. Invariably the demonic force would return and grow in intensity, wearying those of us who were trying to free our Selves from its grip.

I experienced this tension myself, when I entered into the same exploration process for my Self. The tension seemed to proceed from a sense that something profound was left unresolved. What I discovered within my Self and the clients with whom I was working was a dimension of the Self that continues to amaze me.

This awareness put me in mind of the story of the unclean spirit. As the story goes, an unclean spirit leaves a person it had been inhabiting. The spirit wanders about in desolate places looking for someplace to rest, but finds none. Then it says, "Why don't I return to the house I left?" When it returns, it finds the house swept neat—and empty.

Seeing that, the spirit goes out, finds seven other spirits more evil than itself, and brings them all back to inhabit the person together. Though the spirit had been temporarily expelled, and the place it had lived in swept clean, nothing good had been put in its place. When the Spirit returned, the inhabited person was far worse off than he was before (Matt. 12:43–45).

Throughout my own psychological work, and my work with clients, we were aggressively expelling the dark force. Yet there still seemed to be an emptiness of the house, a vacuum within it we were not touching. It was into that vacuum that the Inner Demon kept returning.

Where does that vacuum originate? As we know, during a child's developmental process, when the Inner Other is being created, the child disowns the part or parts of her Self that she understands are unacceptable to her important others. During this disowning process, the child is not only dispossessing her Self of those "unacceptable" parts, she is also creating space within the psyche to accommodate the Inner Other.

When, as an adult, a person goes inward to cast out the Inner Other, and goes no further, a void is created; the parts of the Self that had been disowned are not restored to their proper place. We forget about the inner child, who remains disconnected from and unavailable to the Central I. No matter how forcibly the demon is cast out, the Central I is not restored to health and wholeness, because she does not acknowledge and claim back these long lost parts of the Self.

GHOSTS

Because we buried parts of our Selves when we were children, they are trapped within the conditions of childhood; they are arrested in a child's developmental stage. They perceive their Selves and the world through the eyes of a child. Therefore, their emotional and perceptual states are those of a child and not an adult. This means they perceive :

- the Self as absolutely dependent on the other for survival;
- the important others as infinitely more powerful than themselves;
- themselves as extremely vulnerable to and helpless in relationship to the outside world;
- that others determine their worth; and
- that their ability to process their feelings (especially those that they perceive as going against the parental agenda, i.e., anger, autonomy, and so on) is severely limited and often times very confusing.

As various clients and I made contact with and explored how these inner children experienced reality, these conditions were revealed to us. Therefore, because they came into existence during the childhood development, and because they experienced the world as children do, it seemed appropriate to understand and label these parts of the Self as inner children.

Once I had accepted the reality of these "little people" within our inner world, I reached a new understanding of the story in Matt. 18:2–3.

The chapter opens with the disciples bickering amongst themselves as to who would be the most highly regarded among them by God in the kingdom of heaven. They come to Jesus and ask him to settle it for them. Jesus responds by drawing a child to himself and saying, "Unless you can become like one of these, you will not be able to enter the kingdom."

When I read that chapter before, I could almost hear the stunned silence of his followers. After all, haven't I, haven't we all, struggled to "grow up," to become adults? How could Jesus be telling us to become a child again? I thought that to be a child meant to be at the mercy of others, weak, helpless, dependent. Or, to be silly, mindless, without direction. How wrong I was!

NOT BECOMING THE CHILD YIELDS CHILDISHNESS

The bickering among the disciples demonstrates how unresolved developmental issues become stuck internally and follow people into their adulthood. The disciples were psychologically jockeying with each other to see who would be of more value than the others by getting the "best" position in the kingdom. Implicit in that kind of interpersonal "value-jockeying" is a disbelief in our own intrinsic goodness as people—we attempt to resolve that way of thinking by searching for some external agency, power or person to establish our value through their approval or acceptance.

Somewhere along the process of "growing up," the disciples, like the rest of us, lost trust in the fact that they were loved, and therefore lovable, by their earthly gods—their parents. This inner conflict was then projected onto the Heavenly God, the very God that Jesus had come into the world to represent. What the disciples were missing was that God does not grant a person worth after the fact, but implants that quality at the moment of his or her creation. God could not give the disciples what was already theirs by virtue of the fact that they had been created in His image and likeness in the first place.

Most of us would regard their bickering as a childish display in response to their insecurity about their Selves. Jesus' response to their display, however, is very interesting, as he calls them to become like children. Unless they do so, they will not be able to enter the kingdom of heaven at all. Clearly, Jesus did not mean that they should become childish. So what could Jesus possibly have meant?

As I examined my own inner world and explored with my clients that of their own, we discovered those split-off parts of our Selves resting in the shadows of our psyches. Initially, they revealed themselves in the form of inexplicable anxiety, depression, sadness, intense rage, and aches and pains. When we entered that "space" and began to dialogue with them, we found that they had a lot to say. When we listened and took action on what we heard, we found the inner void became filled and the demon had greater difficulty reentering our lives.

It would seem that what Jesus was trying to say to his disciples and to us is that in order to dwell in the presence of God, old conflicts and inner belief systems must be relinquished. We must change that inner state by reclaiming the lost parts of the Self, the inner children. When Jesus invites us to become like little children, he is inviting us to heal that internal rupture and strife, fill up the ancient void, and crowd out the Inner Other Demon.

THE VIEW FROM ADULTHOOD REVISITED

The problem is not in our creation of this inner world. It serves a very useful purpose during childhood. The problem lies in the fact that this inner world does not evaporate at the end of childhood when it is no longer needed. Instead, it continues on into adulthood to be activated whenever we hit events, situations or people who remind us of the old familial scenes and dynamics.

One of my clients, whom I shall call Lazarus, can help us understand better the energy and interplay of all these inner personae. In a few pivotal sessions, he experienced in a very direct way this inner war of "that which I will to do, I do not. . . ." In a series of two sessions, we explored the inner dynamic that deflected him from fulfilling his goals, and the ways he could stop that deflection.

Lazarus was a person who continually tried to change his Self. He was terrified that others would not like him the way he was and would reject him. He regarded that rejection as tantamount to the destruction of his soul.

Therefore, he tried to figure out who he must become for each individual to like him. As an obvious result, he was not rooted in his own identity, the core of his own being. Rather, he was "outside" himself, changing his identity as a chameleon changes its colors to conform to what he thought the other person wanted him to be at any given moment. If, in Lazarus' eyes, the other person changed how he related to him, Lazarus had to figure out and adjust to that person's new "expectations."

The pain that this chronic loss of identity caused was becoming an unbearable burden. Finally Lazarus realized he was unable to cope by himself, and he entered therapy. Recounted below are portions of two sessions that revealed inner children who were trying to draw his attention to their distress. In these sessions we discovered significant inner dynamics that generated his pain and helped him see and understand what he needed to do to resolve these issues.

As the first of these session unfolds, I sense that there is a deep inner hurt that has not yet been addressed, and suggest to Lazarus that it might be helpful for him to focus, to go into that place of the hurt to explore it. When he indicates that he is focused, I suggest he visualize what he "sees" through his "mind's eye" in that place:

"There's a little boy in there. He exists in an inner void, a place of deprivation and poverty. He's hiding. He's in the corner. (Lazarus indicates the corner diagonally across from him.) He's about ten years old. His name is Andy." (The name of the Inner Child may or may not be that of the adult. Frequently it is not. At this point Lazarus begins to cry.)

When he becomes quiet again, I ask him if he wants to ask Andy to come over to him. He says he does, but Andy appears to be reluctant. He asks Andy why he is so reluctant to accept the invitation. The response is quick and clear, "Because I don't like you. (Long pause) I don't like you not being you—not doing the things you like to do—doing what everyone else is telling you to do. It hurts me when you do that."

Hearing that, Lazarus responds, "Would you like to come over and see if we can work this out?"

(In about ten seconds) "He's over."

Then to Andy he says, "I regret not being myself. I regret listening to what everybody else wants me to be. I'm going to stop doing that. I'm going to do the things I really believe I want to do—to make the decisions that I want to make so that I can be the person I am to be. I want you to be a part of that . . ."

Andy agrees. He wants to be part of that too.

Andy is the equivalent of Bobby's "Turkey." As with Turkey, it is Andy who has been perceived as the enemy and scorned and punished all these years. For Lazarus, facing this part of his Self required a profound humility. It meant admitting that he had abused and battered this Inner Child because he had been so heavily invested in the "security" of his demonic Inner Other.

That is why Jesus says that the person who embarks on this conversion, this turning around of his or her life, needs to be humble like a little child. It means we need to claim the fullness of our being with honesty and without self-aggrandizement or self-deception.

Unless You Become As Little Children

As these sessions unfolded, I saw in what they revealed a new understanding of the entire chapter of Matthew 18, and I have come to call it the Chapter of the Child. Because of these sessions with Lazarus and others like him, I have come to see that Jesus is providing us with a blueprint of a way to be released from the unresolved conflicts that lie buried deep inside. It is these conflicts that keep us in bondage and out of touch with the core identity of our YHWH-ness. Through his outline of inner healing, he helps us be restored to the path of dignity, wholeness, internal peace and positive Self-worth that God originally ordained for us.

To effect that, he is saying we must, as Central I's:

1. face those broken-off pieces of our Selves that are inside us;
2. understand how they see the world;
3. understand, from their point of view, why they react as they do in various situations;
4. admit there has been a failure to acknowledge and help them;
5. take on the role of an unconditionally loving parent by listening, understanding, and validating the feelings and perceptions of the lost parts of the Self;
6. help them experience the world from a point of view other than powerlessness and absolute dependency on the other;
7. become the protector of our inner children;
8. help the Ally realize that the Inner Other is not essential to its survival and that the Central I can take its place;
9. help the instinctual children and the Ally realize they are not as dangerous to each other as they have appeared to be;
10. help them see that they can, in fact, be allies with each other.

When that is achieved, we will find that our deflection from the proper course in our lives will become less frequent and powerful because the Self is in a state of unity, of wholeness within itself. When that happens, there is little room for the law of Sin to wield its power over the Soul.

In his engagement with Andy, Lazarus has taken several steps toward this inner reconciliation. Instead of ignoring or overriding the pain that he had been experiencing throughout his adult life, he finally stopped and faced the underlying meaning of it by discovering the little boy hiding in the inner place of void, deprivation and poverty. Having done so, he has fulfilled condition #1.

When Andy is reluctant to respond, and Lazarus asks him the reason for his reticence, he enters into steps 2 and 3. He is inviting Andy to show him the world as Andy experiences it, and explain what makes him react to it the way he does. Further, by accepting the truth of Andy's responses, Lazarus is being the "good" parent by listening to, understanding and validating what Andy is telling him (#5). Finally, when he says he regrets that he has been dishonoring the Self, he is admitting the failure to acknowledge and help Andy throughout the years (#4). As Lazarus proceeds in his inner healing process, he will have opportunities to fulfill the other steps outlined above.

FIND THE LOST SHEEP

At one point, Jesus asks his disciples, "If a person has a flock of sheep and one gets lost, wouldn't that person leave the flock to fend for itself while he goes to find the sheep that is lost and in danger?" (Matt. 18:12). When Lazarus goes to "look for" Andy, he must visit a place of "void, deprivation, and poverty", Andy's habitation for all these years. It's as if he were entering the hills and dry places to find the one lost sheep that must be found if the flock is to be restored to completeness.

Lazarus emerges from that desolate place bearing with him the lost one of his "flock." To this Jesus says, "Doesn't the sheepherder rejoice more over the found sheep than over the rest of the flock that never was lost? It is not the will of my Father that one of the little ones should perish." Carrying that part of his Self with him out of the dark place into the light of day brings for Lazarus and any of us who find that lost one inside a great deal of relief, peace and joy. When we do that, we become great in the kingdom of heaven.

Jesus reveals the source of that greatness when he says that whosoever receives one of the little ones receives him, the Christ, the IAM incarnate. Thus, when the hurt wells up from the ancient place of pain and we face the meaning of it in the healing of our inner Self, we are receiving the Christ as the Incarnate IAM. People who are committed to reintegrating the lost part of their Selves into the totality of their being and consciousness are working at being in the fullness of their IAM-ness as it is bestowed upon them by God in their creation. That is their greatness in the eyes of God, to be who they are.

THAT WHICH I WILL TO DO, I DO NOT

In another session, it became apparent that Lazarus' Child was very much a part of an event that had occurred a few weeks after the initial session. Again, when Andy was brought into the conversation, there was the same clarity and honesty that threw considerable light onto Lazarus' conflict.

Lazarus described how he had gotten lost on his way to a regular sharing meeting with a group of men with whom he had a long association. He knew the exits on the Interstate, but kept making mistakes, getting more and more lost until it was too late for him to make the meeting.

It needs to be noted that whenever Lazarus talked about Dick and Harry, two of the men in the group, he complained about how frustrated and angry he felt with them. He seemed to be the one who always invested in the relationship, pursuing them and receiving little, if anything, in return. I had often challenged him as to why he persisted in the investment. He agreed that it was a waste of time but continued anyway.

After he described what had happened to him, I suggested that he was getting some kind of message from his unconscious, as though there were something he was not acknowledging.

I suspected there was an Inner Child involved, so I asked Lazarus where his Inner Child was. He immediately became aware of Andy's presence within him. He asked Andy, "What were you aware of on our way to the meeting?"

From his inner space, Andy responded, "We were crossing the bridge, going on Route 80. I was aware of my anger; your anger. I don't like being with them! I'm bored when I'm around them. Neither one of them is interested in opening up to us. All they want is small talk. I'm always disappointed because we never get near anything that is interesting with these two guys. I didn't want you to go. And I was angry at you for not listening! I just decided I wasn't going to let you do that to me!"

Andy, as the feeling/perceptual aspect of Lazarus, was tired of being ignored and overridden. He was simply not going to let it happen again. Lazarus was going to listen whether he wanted to or not. The problem, though, was that Lazarus still didn't understand the true dynamics of the situation. Getting lost wasn't just about the meeting, it was about Lazarus not listening to his feelings and perceptions. When Lazarus took the time and made the effort to understand the meaning of getting lost, he was able to discover its underlying significance. However, this decision did not go unnoticed by the other Inner Child, the one who was invested in conforming to the agenda and demands of the Inner Other Demon.

DESPISE NOT ANYONE OF THESE LITTLE ONES

At the end of the interchange, Lazarus asked Andy what his response was to what had happened. Andy answered that he was happy and relieved that Lazarus has finally acknowledged and heard him. But even as Andy was responding, Lazarus told me he was feeling intense anxiety, and that Andy was fading. He asked Andy what was happening, and Andy said that there was someone inside who didn't want Lazarus to hold on to what had been acknowledged.

Andy informed Lazarus that the Demon had been aroused, and was causing him to fade. Lazarus immediately responded by saying, "Get out of here! I don't want you between me and my little boy anymore. . . . That feels better. He's clearer again. But I'm still feeling some anxiety even though Andy seems to be back."

The specific function of anxiety is to alert the Self to an event that threatens its well-being. Thus, the anxiety that Lazarus was experiencing indicated that some part of his true Self perceived danger. Since it arose at the precise time that Lazarus was considering changing long standing patterns of relating to others, it would seem changing those patterns is what was generating the anxiety.

At this point, I suggested to Lazarus that a part of his Self felt threatened. He emphatically agreed with that: "I feel the threat! But if I'm listening to Andy, why I should be feeling all this anxiety? After all, isn't listening to Andy really listening to my inner truth?"

It must be remembered here that the Inner Other, the demon, is not a part of the Self. It is something that resides within the psychic space, but is a transplant from the outside world. It is not a part of, and does not flow from the energy of the IAM, the Ego. Therefore, we must not only consider the activity of the Inner Other, the demon. We must also look for the part of the Self that is connected to the demon, the Child-Allied-with-the-Inner-Other, who would perceive changing the dynamics of relationships as a refusal to listen to the Inner Other, and therefore a threat.

It is as if we are all on trip to the land of Oz. We're all Dorothys, trying to find our way home to love and wholeness. The Inner Other is the Wizard, hiding behind curtains, telling us lies and dealing in illusions. Andy (or Turkey), the Child of Instinct, is like the Scarecrow, following his heart but never quite believing in himself because he "hasn't got a brain." And the Child-Allied-with-the-Inner-Other is the Cowardly Lion, urging us to go along with the status quo before we find our Selves in real danger. It isn't until these characters pull back the curtains and then reveal the Wizard to be a charlatan that they collect the rewards of their journey (which, as we all know, were inside themselves all along).

I told Lazarus that Andy was his inner truth, but that there was another part who believed in another "truth," which contradicted Andy's. It is the piece of his Self who listens to and believes what the demon says. This Child-Allied-with-the-Inner-Other believes his existence is dependent upon the approval and acceptance of the demon.

I then suggested that Lazarus ask Andy if he knew the part of his Self who was feeling this anxiety, and if so, could he take Lazarus to see him. Andy agreed.

Lazarus described what he saw in that inner place. "He's way deep inside, a long way from here. He's taking my hand. We're passing through a long tunnel or hallway. It is very dark and almost mysterious . . . We're coming to a room, like a throne room. There is a boy on a throne. Andy says this is the one who doesn't like doing what Andy is having me do."

Lazarus asked the new boy what his name was. He replied that his name was Billy (which "coincidentally" was Lazarus' father's name). Lazarus asked Billy why he was feeling all this anxiety. Billy said that he was afraid that if Lazarus let go of his friends Dick and Harry, he would be all alone.

NONE OF THESE LITTLE ONES SHALL BE LOST

Billy is the Inner Child who is highly invested in the old order. Because of that, many believe this part of the Self to be the Inner Demon, a mistake that Lazarus almost made. Many others regard this part of the Self as the enemy, because it appears to contradict our response to the Inner Child. Jesus, however, tells us to not neglect any of his little ones for there is a direct connection between them and the Heavenly Parent. Indeed, it must be remembered that Billy is as much a part of the IAM energy, in the image and likeness of God, as Andy and as Lazarus. Thus, it is important that none of the little ones be lost—including this one.

Thus, if we mistake him for the demon and try to cast him out, then that aspect of the Self is being abused as Andy had been abused earlier. To prevent that from happening, it is necessary that Lazarus recognize Billy as a true part of his Self who deserves honor, respect, understanding and love just like any other true part of the Self.

However, in my experience, this is the most difficult part of the inner healing process. The image of going through winding passages and tunnels that lead to a deep enclosed place is common when others are attempting to encounter this part of their Self. It suggests that this part of the Self is deeply buried to protect himself from discovery and change. Experience has shown that getting that part of the Self to let go of the demonic force is very difficult. But with persistence and, often times, firmness, it can be accomplished.

Unless Lazarus can change the investment Billy has in maintaining the old arrangement, Billy will always exert an unrelenting energy to return Lazarus to that system. It is an energy that could exhaust him in fighting it. If, however, Billy's energy can be transformed to one of unity and cooperation with the rest of the Self, that exhausting fight could end and that energy could be put to more constructive use.

In order to understand more fully how that needs to be effected, we must explore the place of the Central I in the healing process.

❧12❧
The Master of the House

THE CHOICE MAKER

In order for the demons to be cast out and the inner children to be restored to their rightful place in the Self, there has to be an organizing principle. That principle is the Central I referred to in chapter eight. This is the part of the Self that looks outward as well as inward, receiving information from both those realms; she makes decisions and takes action based on that information. As we have seen, however, the information the Central I receives from the inner world can be confusing, causing her to act in ways and have beliefs about her Self and the world that are not in the Self's best interest.

The inner sources of this baffling and, at times, destructive information have been the focus of our consideration up to this point. Once we, as Central I's, know the meaning and significance of the confusing information we receive from the inner world of the psyche, we find ourselves with previously unavailable choices to be made. The question that now stands before us is whether we're willing to make new choices based on new information, or whether we'll fall back to the "safe" old choices.

WORKING OUT THE PARADOX

As humans, we are paradoxes. On the one hand, we exist in the Self-aware state of IAM-ness, outside of time and space in the eternal, non-material now. Clustered around that pure state of being in the unchangeable, outside-of-time center of IAM-ness, are a changing series of events along an ever-changing continuum of time. As these events impinge upon us, stimulation states are created. These, in turn, evoke a conscious awareness of our Selves. So, although at the very center of our IAM-ness, we stand outside of time and space, we need the ever-continuing change of events in time and space to arouse these stimulation

DIAGRAM #1

I AM Consciousness

states. That arousal makes it possible for the eternal, non-material IAM-ness to come alive, to glow and throb with the light of Self-awareness (see diagram #1).

In order for us to operate within the time/space continuum, we possess certain God-given tools by which we process what happens to us. Each event we pass through as eternal, non-material IAMs will:

1. enhance the IAM state;
2. endanger the IAM state; or
3. be neutral to the IAM state.

The function of the Central I is to weigh incoming information and determine an "appropriate" response. This does not happen all at once, but through a series of steps.

When any event occurs, there is a prethought process that begins immediately. That is, before we have any thoughts about what is happening, we have feelings. The feelings produce an awareness that what is happening will either enhance, endanger, or be neutral to the IAM.

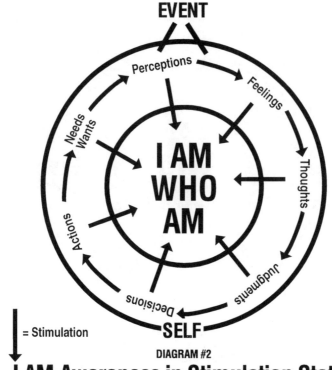

DIAGRAM #2

I AM Awareness in Stimulation States

Feeling states fall into two general categories: the warning and the well-being feeling states. The warning feelings states arouse us to prepare for danger to the IAM, and mobilize us to cope with whatever that danger may be. Among the warning feelings are: anger, fear, anxiety, sadness, frustration, emptiness, or guilt. When we speak of emotional hurt or pain, we are referring to this category of feelings.

The well-being feeling states inform the IAM that it is not in danger (neutrality), or that the IAM is in some way being positively enhanced. Among the well-being feelings are: happiness, joy, emotional warmth, security, peace, and wholeness (see diagram #2).

Once the Central I is aroused into a state of awareness about a given event, she then enters into a cognitive state. The first level of cognition is the processing of the data it receives through the senses, i.e., what it sees, hears, or touches. As more data or circumstances around the event come in, the second level of cognition begins: integrating the data received within the experience of the Central I. Integration means that we admit that the event is, in fact, happening. "I am feeling _____ because such and such is happening." As this process of data gathering, connecting and integrating proceeds, the feelings may intensify, diminish or change.

As the data-gathering process goes on, we move into the third level of the process: judgment. The Central I must evaluate the accuracy, completeness and appropriateness of the sources of her information. She then makes a judgment as to whether or not to continue in the event, and what kind of response is needed. Once a judgment is made, we must then act on it. This process of experiencing, evaluating, arriving at judgments and taking action is called reality testing.

On paper, this process would seem to be rather straightforward. Reality testing, however, is a complex, multifaceted and multilayered function the Self possesses as a way of both surviving and living. It is a function the infant does not possess and to which the small child has limited access. It is, rather, a function that requires psychological readiness at progressive stages in the developmental process; the assistance of parental figures to teach us the various skills that are part of the reality-testing process; and our normal life experience. If there is any flaw in how we are initiated into this process, that flaw becomes a part of our unconscious.

WE ARE NOT ANGELS

Often, that flaw causes the Central I to deny that events are actually happening. The reasoning is, "If I can deny that this event is happening to me, I don't have to deal with its impact on my life. I can avoid what I am feeling about this event, and I can avoid taking action in response to that event." Denying "reality" becomes a perfect way to avoid claiming the disowned "bad" parts of the Self. However, when the Central I responds to events in this way, the loss of the ability of the Self to participate in the human time/space continuum deprives him of the stimulation states he needs to maintain an adequate sense of consciousness (see diagram #3).

To fortify these personal attitudes about our Selves and the flight from participation in the time/space continuum, we build social and cultural mores and laws that fortify this internal arrangement. Religion and theological systems are not exempt from this process. In fact, they form a very powerful backup to this kind of internal system of denial.

Within the Roman Catholic tradition, for instance, there are traditions of asceticism that try to convince us that perfection, in part, consists in the avoidance and/or denial of the fact that we exist in time and space. Roman Catholics, however, do not have the corner on the market when it comes to this kind of religious attitude. There are certainly other religious

EVENT

Perceptions Garbled

Feelings Denied

Needs Wants Denied

I AM Awareness Shrinks

Thoughts Confused

Actions Hesitant Incomplete

Judgments Blurred

Decisions Muddled

ˌSELFˌ

= Muted Stimulation

DIAGRAM #3

The Breakdown of Stimulation States

traditions—such as focusing on heaven as the reward while minimizing the importance of the here and now—that try to convince us that we should somehow transcend the time/space reality, or that time/space is irrelevant and/or dangerous and involvement in it should be avoided at all costs.

This point of view makes it appear that we are angels, who are to operate either as though time/space does not exist, or to fix our vision on the afterlife with little or no consideration for what is happening to us or others around us now. We were not created as angels who exist in another dimension. *This* is our dimension, the one of time and space.

IF YOUR BROTHER SINS AGAINST YOU

One way that many of us have developed to deny reality is to deny our own feelings. One feeling that we in this culture have particular difficulty with is anger. Most of us learn very early that the expression of anger is not allowed. As a result, we learn quickly to disassociate from it.

This lesson was driven home to me in the following event: I was working with a married couple whose relationship was in serious trouble.

I listened to the wife describe what happened whenever the two had a disagreement. She would attempt to talk with her husband about it. Invariably, the disagreement would escalate with him shouting and getting red in the face; it would end with him stomping out of the house, slamming the door and disappearing into the barn. He would return after several hours as though nothing had happened; there was no acknowledgment that there had been any disagreement.

I asked the husband if he agreed with his wife's description. He responded that he did. I then asked him why he dealt with his anger that way, never expecting the response that he gave. He said, "I never get angry." After I was able to regain my power of speech, I asked him what anger meant to him. Being the church-going Catholic he was, he said, "It is a sin to be angry. So, I never get angry!"

This is obviously an extreme example of the denial of anger, but it shows well how much difficulty many of us can have with it. Whether our distrust of it comes from our family of origin, from our own confusing and overwhelming experience of it, and/or from our religious beliefs, many of us have deep problems relating to and acting on these feelings.

Anger alerts the Self that it is being violated. If properly understood and used, it is designed to motivate us to protect our IAM-ness.

In point of fact, in the same chapter of Matthew we have been exploring, Jesus (18:15–17) admonishes his disciples to confront a brother who has violated us. Jesus was telling his followers to respect, listen to and act on their anger. He goes on to say that if the brother ultimately cannot own the wrong that has been done, the person who has been wronged should treat the wrongdoer as though he is a Gentile and a tax collector.

In the context of the day, Gentiles and tax collectors were the most repulsive kind of persons there could be, and were to be avoided at all costs. These persons were to be excluded from the life of the individual who was wronged as well as from the community at large. Therefore, so fully must the individual respect her anger, that, in protection of the Self, she is to totally disconnect from the wrongdoer who demonstrates that he cannot respect the individual's being.

Jesus finishes his comment on anger saying, "Anything you bind on earth shall be bound in heaven, and whatever you loose on earth, shall be loosed in heaven." In other words, God will back us up if we follow through on the judgment our feelings and perceptions in truth bring to us. Rather than following our learned responses to anger, namely to ignore, disregard, disown, or run away from it, we are to honor it and to use it to protect our being in the image and likeness of God.

Listening to our feelings, however, can be tricky business because of what we have learned about our feelings, and the distrust and fear we have of them as a result. We may have feelings that are generated out of our subconscious, and we do not fully understand them and why they are occurring. However, there is a fundamental law of feelings that I've come to realize: "Every feeling has a reason to be." Our task is to honor the feeling and to resolve the situation, internal or external, to which that feeling is alerting us.

THE TWO REALITIES

We as human beings constantly deal with two realities. One is the outside world, the world we physically inhabit. The other is the internal reality, in which the Central I, the demon, and the inner children interact. Because many people are not aware that this very real and intense inner reality even exits, they think their reactions are rooted in, and responding to, external events. Therefore, they attach significance and meaning to external events that may have nothing to do with what they're really feeling.

Here's an example of this confusion about the difference between the inner and outer realities: Once, at a group session, Lazarus began to cry about something, and he felt deeply embarrassed. People become embarrassed when they perceive that something they have done (in this case, crying) will devalue them in the eyes of others. Lazarus assumed that people in the group would think less of him because he cried.

I asked the group if that was the case. They said, in fact, that they respected him for being able to let his feelings show. That response helped Lazarus realize that his feeling reaction was not in response to the people sitting around him, but to someone inside. I asked him who would devalue him if he acknowledged and expressed his feelings. This prompted him to switch from examining the external reality to examining the internal reality. When he did that, he realized it was his Father-Demon humiliating him for his tears. Once he realized that, he was able to confront that inner voice, and was relieved of his embarrassment.

FREEDOM TO CHOOSE

Once we understand that there is an inner world that intrudes into and disrupts our ability to remain on course in our lives, and we become aware of the messages that emanate from that inner world, freedom of choice is opened up to us. We do not have to be helpless to the power of sin and darkness in us. We have, instead, the choice to process what is happening inside us and to make new choices based on that information.

We have the freedom to choose to whom we will listen in the inner world, the light of the IAM or the darkness of the Inner Other Demon. In our freedom to choose between the Power of Light or the Power of Darkness, there are profound ramifications. As we struggle to make that decision, Jesus encourages us to use him as the light (John 12:35–36), so that the darkness does not overtake us. When we walk in that darkness we do not know where we go. But if we believe in him as the light, then we will become the children of light. If within, we are in the daylight—the fullness of our identity—we will not stumble. If, however, there is night inside us, we will stumble, because we cannot see where we go (John 11:9–10).

Saying these things, he addresses us as Central I's with the ability to reality test, that is, to know and choose the true light of the unfractured IAM. Part of the challenge by Jesus to the Central I is to examine whether or not we are following the truth of the true IAM or the falsehood of the demon. If we can see where we are going in life because we are lit up from within by the light of the IAM that is in each of us, then we walk the way of the Lord. If, however, we stumble about because we exist in the nothingness of our internal demons, then we walk in its darkness and lies.

LOVE OF DARKNESS

Satan's hold upon us is tight. Its darkness breeds darkness. We become lost in its darkness believing we have found light. Thus, we are very reluctant to let go of it; we hang onto it for dear life. Jesus the Christ knows us well. He says that we love the darkness and prefer it over the light. But the darkness generates evil deeds. Then, whoever does evil has to remain in the dark so that his evil deeds will not be seen. But whosoever does what is true comes into the light so that his deeds may be seen by all (John 3:19–21).

A significant part of the reason people choose the darkness of the demon rather than the light granted to them is reflected in this parable that Jesus tells:

A rich man was about to fire his steward because of incompetence. The lord summons his servant before him, confronts the servant with his ineptitude and orders him to present an accounting so his services might be terminated. The man is panic stricken at the thought of being fired from his job, for he realizes that he has no other identity. To do anything else is incomprehensible to him.

The steward realizes that if he is fired, he will have nowhere to stay. Therefore, he thinks, if he can make his master's debtors beholden to him, he at least could rotate among them so that he would have a place to stay and something to eat. So he summons each one of his master's debtors to him and he lowers each of their bills. When the lord realizes what his servant has done, he commends him for his shrewdness in taking care of himself (Luke 16:1–10).

Jesus is sketching out the demonic system in this story. This parable clearly illustrates the entire dynamic of what happens to those of us who get so lost in pleasing our demons, we do not have access to the light of the true God that is reflected in our own inner light.

The steward in the parable starts where we all do, as children who are on the threshold of taking over the goods of our own life. We are not yet our own masters, for we are still subject to our parenting figures (internal and external). We are told of our incompetence in managing our affairs, or that is what we think we're being told, so we come to believe this about our Selves. We search frantically for ways to offset what we believe to be the loss of stewardship over our own lives and identities.

To make up for the loss of Self, we try to ingratiate others to our Selves in hopes of filling our inner emptiness through the false sense of substance that is gained through the approval, approbation and acceptance of our pseudo-debtors.

What is interesting here is that the steward receives in the kind he gives. The system only works if others are indebted to the rich man (the demon) in the same way the steward is. The person who seeks the adulation and acceptance of his fellows, gives back to others, in kind, approval and adulation by appearing to have the power to write off the master's debt. As long as everyone plays the same game, and believes that substance and worth are bestowed by the approbation of others, the system works. But it is all an illusion.

GOD VS. MAMMON

People who subscribe to this illusion think they are being granted a life that actually is not there. Believing they get what they seek, they think they serve God. However, it is impossible to serve, to respond to the game plan of the false god of the psyche, and also to the will of the true God. Jesus alludes to this when he says a person cannot have two masters. That person will either hate the one and love the other or be devoted to one and despise the other. He says one cannot serve both God and the god of mammon (of possessions, of riches, of appearances) (Luke 16:13).

This is so because the fundamental law of the Demon rests upon the act of giving up one's IAM-ness. The fundamental law of the true Creator-God is that each of us claim the IAM-ness that is our gift and birthright. We cannot be true to that and still give it up. It is like bringing spiritual matter and antimatter together. When that happens, the being disintegrates.

In Matt. 18:8–10, Jesus instructs us, if there is a part of our being— a hand, a foot, an eye—that causes us to miss the mark of our life, then we need to cut it off. This means we are to cast away from us the power that tries to seduce us into its orbit, thereby obliterating the Law of God which is to exist in the fullness and well-being of God within us.

Jesus appeals to the Central I to cast out the demons and return the lost parts of the Self to the center of our lives. Often, when we suffer aches and pains and illnesses, when we are confused by feelings and/or behaviors that seem to come out of nowhere, it is these lost parts of our being who are trying to warn us that we are missing the mark when we listen to the demons. In balance to that, Jesus warns us not to neglect the Ally in this process of conversion: "Do not despise anyone of these little ones . . ." (Matt. 18:10), for this part of the Self must be healed also.

DISCERNMENT

With this new knowledge about the meaning of the messages from the inner world, we are now better able to differentiate between the true Creator-God and the false god of our psyche. Throughout the Gospels, there are a variety of images and metaphors that represent the Central I as the decision-making part of the Self. Exploring them might help us understand the ramifications for us if we fall back in fear or laziness to the old demonic system; and so that we might, instead, motivate our Selves to harness these new awarenesses to make new choices and decisions that are growth-filled and bring us more into harmony with our Selves and others.

THE SOWER OF THE SEEDS

The struggle over which internal choice each Central I will ultimately make is shown in the two parables of the sown seed: There is a farmer who goes out to sow his seed. Some of the seed falls along the path; some of it is gobbled up by birds. Still other seed falls on rocky ground; as soon as it springs up, it has no soil and moisture, and it shrivels up under the intense heat of the midday sun. Some other seed falls among thorns that grow faster than the wheat; the wheat is choked to death by the thorns. But other seed falls on good and fertile ground and brings forth an abundance many times richer than what had originally been planted (Matt. 13:1–30).

There are those who hear the word that saves but do not understand it. Because they have so thoroughly given their Selves over to the Evil One, the Good Word is incomprehensible to them. As a result, reformation of their inner world is totally unavailable to them. This is the seed that falls on the path and is trampled underfoot.

There are those who hear the word and understand it. They receive what they hear with joy, but they are not rooted in their Selves. The word remains with them for a while. But they are empty inside and cannot give up their attachment to the word of the Dark One. As a result, when they are tested by trials and tribulations, they fall away. This is the seed that falls on rocky ground.

Then there are those who hear the word but have been seduced into believing that their worth is wrapped up in what others think of them. As a result, they are so preoccupied with how they appear to the world, that the word gets choked out of their life. That is the seed that is sown among thorns.

Then there are those who hear the word, understand it, take it to heart and live their lives by it. They live in integrity without compromise to the Demonic One. As a result, they are filled with the goodness of the IAM, existing as the reflected light of the YHWH as their unique manifestation of the Godhead in the created world. That is the seed that falls on good soil and yields in great abundance.

A second parable is the landowner who sows good seed in the field. But an enemy comes while everyone is sleeping and sows weeds in the same field. As the crop comes to maturity, the weeds contaminate the good wheat. The servants come and inform the landowner of what has happened. He assures them that only good seed has been used and that an enemy had come and defiled the planting. So they ask him what they should do. He tells them not to try to uproot the weeds because that would destroy the wheat as well. Instead, they are to wait until the crop ripens. Then the reapers will gather the weeds first and burn them. After that, they will gather up the wheat and store it in the barn.

Explaining the parable, Jesus tells his friends that the sower is the Son of man; the field is life; the good seed is the children of the kingdom; the weeds are the children of the Evil One; the harvest is the end of time; the reapers, angels. The children of the Evil One, the cause of all sin, will be gathered and burnt at the end of time. The children of the kingdom will then shine like the sun in the kingdom of the Holy Parent (Matt. 13:24–43).

In life choices the individual makes, the reality and activity of the Inner Other Demon (biblically, the Evil One) figure prominently in the struggle these parables paint about life. Jesus says that when anyone hears the word of the kingdom and does not understand it, "the Evil One comes and snatches away what is sown in his heart." The Evil One is clearly an enemy who dwells within; one who has enough power to evade and, if given the chance, to obliterate a person's wellspring of spiritual life.

We can override the Evil One by choosing not to compromise our soul to the seductions, manipulations and dictates of the Inner Demon. However, when we do, like Jesus, honor the integrity of our uniqueness in the image and likeness of God, we will, like him, suffer at the hands of the Dark Power from within or without. But if we are steadfast, like he was, in our refusal to capitulate, we will be resurrected also.

THE INVIOLABILITY OF FREE WILL

Our ability to override the power of darkness implies free will—that is, because we now have options, we can freely choose either the reality of light offered by God through his Son Jesus or the reality of the darkness offered us by the demonic force.

Jesus points out to us the responsibility each person must take for his or her ultimate life decisions. He addresses that personal responsibility and authority when he talks about his coming into the world to be light to those who desire not to remain in the darkness. It is our choice that will be our judge, not the Son of God. We either resonate with the truth that is contained within his word or we do not. If we do, that is our salvation; if we do not, that is our damnation (John 12:46–50).

It is clear in this saying (and within the entire context of salvation history) that it is the will of God that no person's freedom of choice be overlooked or canceled out. On the other hand, the choices we make determine what we will receive. If we choose the light, that is what we will find in the present as well as in the eternal afterlife. If we choose darkness, then it is darkness that will be given to us now and after death in respect for our choices. The light will be our judge, if the light is chosen; the darkness will be our judge if the darkness is chosen.

In his kindness, Jesus, as Word, reminds us what we will get with each kind of choice. If we choose the Evil One to be our identity, then we will reap its rewards—fiery pain of inner emptiness, loneliness, entrapment, and suffocation. If we choose the inner true identity that was essential to the creative act of our individual humanity, the reward is ". . . to shine like the sun," to live a life of brilliant light that emanates from within and to dwell in the land of the Holy Parent where light meets light.

SAND OR ROCK

In Matt. 7:24–27, Jesus tells the story of the wise person who builds her house on rock compared to the one who builds his house on sand. In this story, the wise or foolish ones are images for the part of the Self, the Central I, who is called upon to make the fundamental decisions about life.

The foolish one is the Central I that chooses, instead of his Self as the reference point in his life, the voice of the Inner Other Demon. The foundation for his Self is built upon sand. He has no substance because he shifts in response to any force (the opinion of others) that exerts itself upon the sand. The various storms that come and go as a part of normal living erode the house of the Self from its very foundations. The result is that the normal buffeting from life causes this house of the Self to collapse with a great noise.

The wise one, on the other hand, is the Central I of a person who chooses the fundamental proposition of the love of Self. This person builds upon the rock of her own personal substance. She knows who she is. The opinions of others do not affect her inner sense of goodness, fullness and substantiality. No storm of life can prevail against her for she is solid in her Self no matter what her interaction with the outer world may bring.

This is the love of the IAM-ness of the Self and the love of others as IAMs that Jesus teaches. If, however, I do not love and respect my own IAM-ness, I do not possess the fundamental wherewithal, the base, from which I can love others as IAMs. I am empty in the core of my being. It is easy for me to be crushed in my interaction with the outside world if that is my inner attitude. Chris, Dana, Abel and Lazarus, as Central I's, began to examine what was happening to them and embark on their psycho-spiritual journey in therapy because of the collapse of their shaky inner foundations. Once they entered it, they found they had to rearrange the fundamental alliances they had made with their demons and to reclaim the parts of their Selves they had lost along the way of growing up.

A KINGDOM DIVIDED

The destructiveness of this alliance of the Central I with the Inner Demon is sketched in Luke 11:14–23: "Every kingdom divided against itself is laid waste, and house falls upon house. When a strong man, fully armed, guards his own palace, his goods are in peace; but when one stronger than he assails him and overcomes him, he takes away the man's armor in which he trusted, and divides the spoil."

Within the psyche, the demon assails the true ruler of the realm of the Self, the Central I, removes it from power and strips it of its armor—the feelings, thoughts, perceptions and judgment through which the Self is protected against the loss of his identity. The demon removes from the Self, to a greater or lesser extent, the right to stand up for himself, to defend himself against those who knowingly or unknowingly rob him of his rights.

On the other hand, the person who remains strong in her Self, claiming all the parts of her Self—her feelings, perceptions, thoughts and judgment—remains invincible in the core of her soul. She is at peace within her own domain. No matter what may be raging outside her Self, within there is peace, calm and protectedness.

∞13∞

Inner Reconciliation

TURNING AWAY FROM THE ABUSER

What keeps the Central I in the power of the Inner Other Demon, dividing the kingdom of the Self against his Self, laying him waste? The Child Ally is terrified to let go of the Inner Other as his reference point for survival. But what gives that Inner Child so much power within the organization of the Self?

The original political arrangement under which the Ally was created gave him that primacy. As long as the Ally is lost in the realm of the unconscious, he exercises great power over the Central I from that place. As a result, whether we like it or not, or whether we know it or not, the laws by which he operates take us over and rule us, as Paul complains with such poignancy in Romans 7.

If we are to be freed from the profoundly damaging grip of this internal political arrangement, then, in the spirit of verse 10 of Matthew, it is required of us that we come to appreciate the point of view of this Inner Child as much as that of our "Andys." We must appreciate where he (or she) is coming from and communicate our wish to understand him. We must seek him out and return him to the fold. Once those children who have been lost inside are found, there can be great rejoicing, greater than for those who were not lost.

In Lazarus' case, the Ally's point of view began to manifest itself when, as a result of my challenge to him, Lazarus began to give up his focus on what he thought were the rigid expectations of others, and began to consider his own needs, wants and feelings. Billy became very threatened by that and revealed his existence through anxiety. From Billy's perspective, if the laws of the inner others were given up, his life was being threatened. The only way this inner conflict between Andy and Billy-the-Ally-of-the-Demon could be resolved was to demonstrate to Billy that the Inner Other Demon was not necessary for his survival.

The Ally (Billy) has minimal access to outside reality because he is so bound up in his relationship with the Inner Other, the demon of the psyche. There is little room for new information about the world to penetrate the inner place where he resides. The result is that his perceptions of what is happening to the Self remain largely static and negative, determined by the dictates of the static and negative Inner Demonic Force.

It has become apparent to me in the past few years that, in order for this inner situation to change, the Central I must make a conscious effort to carry these new insights and awarenesses of experience into the deepest recesses of the psyche to this Child who is bound so tightly to the Inner Other Demon.

OBSOLESCENCE

The primary focus of that reeducation is to get the Ally to see that his relationship with the Inner Other is now obsolete. Yes, the Inner Other was at one time essential to our development and survival. Some of the "laws" and rules of conduct that developed were necessary and appropriate for us to learn if we were to be able to function in the interpersonal world.

There were, however, some "laws" we incorporated during childhood (in the persona of the Inner Other) that contain lies about the Self in all his parts, about the world of others, and about the demon itself. If we listen to these lies and laws, they destroy us from inside. One such law is the belief we have explored so many times in other places in this work: "You are irrelevant and worthless unless you are accepted and approved of by others." Through these kinds of laws, the Inner Other makes value judgments about who we are. That's when the Inner Other moves from a constructive presence in our inner world to a destructive one. When we carry these kinds of laws into adulthood, the Inner Other becomes the Inner Demon.

Furthermore, it must be noted that the laws were learned within the limited environment of the family of origin, to be applied to specific persons in that specific environment. These laws help us function, negotiate and survive within the environment of the family of origin. For instance, a child who finds herself with a violent, alcoholic parent who humiliates family members whenever he can learns definite laws governing relationships and survival.

As we begin to move out of our limited family environment, we often apply these "laws" to the world in general. The child who grew up in the alcoholic family expects all relationships to be based on nastiness, violence and victimization. The laws she learned about how people relate, and how she is related to, will then be applied to most, if not all, of her relationships.

Likewise, the roots of Billy's existence and his intense relationship with the Inner Other can be traced back to Lazarus' childhood. The laws he learned did help him cope within the family. But now, through Billy's influence, they were being applied to Lazarus's adult world, where they didn't belong.

TEMPTATIONS WILL COME

Lazarus was a child who was born late in his parents' life, and was often left to fend for himself. (These are impressions and experiences *he* had of his parents which may or may not be historically accurate.) His mother and father demonstrated little positive regard toward him. This emotional and psychological passivity seemed to be particularly true of his mother. He yearned to be validated by her so he could feel good about his Self, but his wish rarely came true. He came to believe that he would never be all right, never be lovable unless that nonresponsive, important other would someday validate his worth with some kind of positive response. That primal experience of nonvalidation and yearning came to be one of the dynamics encapsulated in the persona of Billy. As a result, Billy, stuck in that place of nonvalidation and unlovability, had a very intense relationship with his Internalized Mother.

On the other hand, Lazarus' father had very rigid rules and expectations for him. For instance, when the family knelt down to say the Rosary, if Lazarus did not maintain a particular posture throughout the entire recitation, his father would hit him on the back of his legs—with a switch that Lazarus had had to go out and cut himself. Lazarus concluded that if he did not live up to his father's expectations, he would be humiliated and regarded as worthless by his father. He came to believe that he was not lovable because of his inadequacies. He thought that if he could fulfill his father's expectations, he could reverse the negative paternal judgment. He would be approved of, and therefore loved, and therefore have worth.

As his inner world developed, the messages Lazarus received from his parents were repeated by his demon: "I know everything about you. I know how incompetent you are. I know how imperfect you are, and therefore how unlovable. I can take away the pain of your imperfection if you follow my rules, if you do everything I tell you . . . be nice to Dick, Harry . . . whomever. . . . Get them to notice you and let you know how much they appreciate what you do for them and how perfect you are at doing it, then you will feel good about your Self. If you slip up in any way, they won't acknowledge you. Then you will feel all those terrible feelings about who you aren't. The only way you can avoid that from happening is if you listen to me and do everything I tell you. If you do that, you will be OK."

This was the "law" Lazarus learned. If he was to "survive," and avoid humiliation, he had to listen very closely to every nuance, verbal and non-verbal, of the other person. By following the law very closely, he was able to "keep his losses" to a minimum. Billy himself adhered in this way to his demon voice, anxiously trying to conform to the very rigid "expectations" of the other person. This kept him constantly waiting to be noticed, affirmed and recognized as a person with worth by anyone and everyone who crossed his path.

Ironically, listening to the Inner Voice was Billy's lifeline. From his perspective, to let go of that voice was to relinquish the power that established his identity in the world. As he put it so eloquently, "If we let go . . . we will be all alone." This translates into, "If we let go of the laws of the Inner Other, we will not know if anyone likes us. If we don't know that, we are in limbo. Without that positive affirmation from without, we are a nobody. If we are a nobody, we will be all alone." He would be left adrift in an ocean of uncertainty about who he was in relationship to others. Thus Lazarus, through Billy, hung onto the demon for dear life.

EXPECTING THE WORST

As Lazarus got older, and through Billy applied to the world in general those laws and rules of relationship that were specific to his mother and father, they became very destructive to him. He constructed a wall between his Self and others. He tried very hard to read what others' expectations of him might be. He would then form his Self according to the expectations he perceived. Because of his guardedness, he was never able to form significant bonds of intimacy with others. This resulted in a deep sense of loneliness. And the continual capitulation or giving over of his Self to what he thought were the expectations of others resulted in the profound pain of the loss of his identity.

The pain had become unbearable and was progressively immobilizing him. He knew he needed to do something to get his life back. The most effective way to do that would be to dialogue with Billy as he had begun to do in the session discussed earlier.

THE ORIGINAL ACHIEVEMENT

The goal of this dialogue with Billy is to help him see that the demon lies and misleads him, and that his existence is not dependent on the demon. However, it requires that we respect "Billy" as much as we respect

"Andy." Admitting the significance of the Ally's help in surviving childhood is often a very powerful way to gain its trust, and therefore access to constructive dialogue.

If this important achievement by this part of the Self is denied by the Central I and the Children of Instinct, the Ally will continue to be perceived as an enemy and adversary. Likewise, the Ally will perceive the Central I and the instinctual children in the same light. That, obviously, can lead only to a stalemate in which neither side can win. If, on the other hand, we are successful at building trust with that part of our Self, it becomes possible for us to begin the necessary reeducation of this part of the Self to help lead him out of his now destructive, distorted relationship with the Inner Other demon.

That does not mean, however, giving in to what he demands. What it does mean is that we listen to what he has to say and be willing to help him get what he needs, if these needs are appropriate. If what he thinks he needs is not appropriate, we must help him see this, and supply him with something less damaging to the Self.

As Lazarus grew up and physically left home, Billy "remained at home" by finding a long succession of people who, like his parents, related to him in a very one-sided way. The result was that Billy never experienced that sense of validation he so yearned for.

The energy of the yearning to be validated was so powerful that Lazarus was obsessed by people who were nonresponders and nonvalidators, people like his "friends" Dick and Harry. His obsession was so strong, that those who did respond and validate him made no impact on him. So, ironically, the very thing that he so assiduously pursued did not even register when it was available. Billy's identity was tied up in the yearning rather than in the getting. For Lazarus to be healed and freed of this conundrum, he would somehow have to help Billy to let go of the yearning, to be satisfied with what he got rather than always concentrating on what he didn't have.

THE REAL CULPRIT

The real source of this destructive power struggle, however, was not Billy but the Inner Other Demon. It was this force who seduced Lazarus into the postures that became his lifestyle. As a result, it was his Inner Despot who constantly and primarily abused him, not Dick and Harry.

Lazarus' goal was to help Billy to understand that his perception—if he gives up these "friends," he will be alone in the world—is not accurate. Quite to the contrary, giving up Dick and Harry would free up the energy invested in these "dead end" relationships; energy that could be reinvested in actual responders and validators.

It is clear that the primary energy that held Billy to his allegiance with the demon was his fear of being alone. Therefore, Lazarus' task was to demonstrate to Billy's satisfaction that stepping out in this new direction would not result in his being a nobody in the world, absolutely alone. In order to do that, Lazarus also had to demonstrate that the demon was not a power that could be relied upon.

LAZARUS: Can you see that you've been duped by the demon and that you don't have to listen to it anymore?

BILLY: Yes, I can see that it has lied to me. But I'm still afraid that there will be nobody there for me.

LAZARUS: Well, I'll be there for you. I am being there for you. I'm listening to you right now, aren't I?

BILLY: Yes.

LAZARUS: Has the demon ever listened to you?

BILLY: No. It only yells at me when Andy or I have done something wrong.

Finally Billy was beginning to face the reality that the demon is unreliable and even the opposite of what Billy hoped it to be. Lazarus is truly listening and validating Billy's concerns. Billy is still worried, however, about being alone. Because of that worry, he is still reluctant to let go of his attachment to the demon. Hearing Billy's concern, Lazarus reassures him that he himself will be the loving, benign, accepting parent that Billy has yearned after but never found. That offer opens up the possibility that he might be able to let go of his attachment to the demon and to move into a relationship with someone different, someone who cares — Lazarus himself.

In the session, Lazarus told Billy, "I just want you to know that I really love you. I've not really understood who fwere up until now. But I'm glad we've met and talked. I know, now, that this is all very difficult for you. I understand that you will continue to have anxiety about this new way of doing things. And I also want to let you know that I pledge that when you are having difficulty, I will come in here to find out what is happening for you so that we can work it out."

Lazarus is doing for Billy what he did for Andy. He's acknowledging who he is and validating what he both feels and needs. By so doing Lazarus himself:

1.   gives Billy what he never experienced from the parents and, as a result, has yearned for ever since;

2. extends the hand of acceptance and love that has been missing in Billy's existence up to this point;

3. offers Billy a commitment to continued support, validation, sensitivity and appreciation for who he is.

Lazarus is claiming back another facet of his IAM-ness and therefore the Word of God as it is manifested in him.

How Often Must I Forgive?

Although there has been an important breakthrough in the relationship between Billy and Lazarus, where Billy and Andy stand in their relationship to each other is still unclear. The next step, then, is to get Billy and Andy to realize that they no longer need to be enemies, but can be friends who can work together for the common good:

LAZARUS:	So Andy, how do you see Billy now?
ANDY:	I see him very differently now. I used to hate him because of what he did to me when he listened to the demon and because he was so afraid of it. But now I understand what happened and why he did what he did.
LAZARUS:	Billy, what do think of that?
BILLY:	That makes me feel a lot better. I don't see Andy as so bad anymore.
LAZARUS:	Well, maybe the two of you don't have to be enemies any longer. As a matter of fact, you can help each other out so that the demons aren't so strong.
BILLY AND ANDY:	We can see that now. But when the demons take over, we have to fight each other.
LAZARUS:	Well, how will it be if I keep a watch out for when that happens? When it does, I'll come in there and help us all figure what's going on. I'll help the two of you not fight each other and, instead, fight what the demons are doing to destroy us. They're saying they think that will work. But I've got to listen to what they're trying to tell me. . . . They're right; I am going to have to listen. But this certainly gives me a much better idea of what goes on inside and what I need to do to resolve it.

Hearing the Lost Sheep Calling Out

When the internal personae are in conflict, the one who perceives himself as the underdog sends out signals to inform the Central I of his distress. Most of us, like Lazarus, don't understand the meaning of these internal communications. Lazarus now has a much better grasp of the meanings of these internal messages. He can now use them to resolve inner conflicts, by being aware of the nature of the communications, going inward to examine what is creating the conflict, and then working it out between his inner children. This will help him live up to his promise to both Andy and Billy to work to understand each of them.

Therefore, it's important that Lazarus be consciously aware of the importance of these communications from within. With that in mind, I asked Lazarus, "What do you think your cues will be to let you know you have to go inside to see what is happening?"

He responded; "Well, a big one is the anxiety. It's clear to me now that when I'm anxious, either Andy or Billy is having difficulty with something that I need to help them resolve."

If we listen to what the inner children are trying to say to us through these kinds of feeling states, we can understand what Jesus means when he says, "I thank you, Holy Parent, that you have hidden these things from those who are wise and understanding and revealed it to the little ones. Such is your wonderful will" (Matt. 11:25–26). When we, like Lazarus, talk with this inner part of our Selves, the Inner Children respond with the same kind of astonishing clarity, integrity, honesty and wisdom we often hear from real children.

The Size of the Flock

As with the "legions" of inner demons that may possess us, it has become apparent that there is often a multitude of inner children, more than the two we have just explored. One client, who was constantly bounced from one inner conflict to another, was able to identify a number of distinct inner children who manifested themselves in the course of our work together. She found, as others did, that when an internal issue manifested itself, such as an anxiety that didn't seem to be attached to anything specific or the emergence of physical muscular tension (a headache or throat tension, for example), moving into a dialogue with that part of the Self often unveiled an Inner Child who revealed herself to be a different entity to ones previously encountered. Or as the dialogdue moves along, as with Lazarus, it became apparent there was another persona involved in what was generating the anxiety.

For this client, in addition to the Ally, there was the Victim Child who perceived herself as always under the thumb of and inferior to the other person; the Shame Child who perceived herself as having no worth whatsoever; the Confused Child who found what was happening both in the internal and outside world so overwhelming and contradictory that she lived in a state of unrelieved confusion; the Guilt Child who believed that anything that went "wrong" was her fault; the Fearful Child who was terrified of making a mistake and, as a result, was always looking over her shoulder to see who might be watching and basically was in a state of chronic immobilization.

In addition to encapsulated feelings states like the ones described above, there can be inner children who are stuck in traumatic events. For instance, if there was sexual abuse, there often is an Inner Child who is frozen in the sexually abusive scene. However, there may be a separate Inner Child(ren) who exist before or after the abuse event(s) also.

These are all children of vulnerability. However, there is usually the Child of Wisdom who knows and says the naked truth about what has been and is going on if she is given the chance to speak. She was repressed during childhood because it was not always in the child's best interest to blurt out exactly what she thought and felt about what was going on. It is this child, though, who, if accessed, allows the Central I to begin to get information about what the inner world is all about and what actions need to be taken to resolve the inner chaos and conflict.

All of these separate inner children are created around a specific time (the "no" period, beginning of going to school), event (birth of a sibling), familial dynamic (alcoholism), or trauma (death, divorce), and/or feeling state (anger, sadness, confusion, guilt, or shame).

Even though many of us share the same characters in our inner mythology, it needs to be noted that each of us creates our own inner landscape peopled by our own inner children. We need to listen to what each of them has to say from each of their own perspectives in that inner world. Listening, we can help them move out of the old scene in which they find themselves trapped to a new one in which they are free.

COMING TO WHOLENESS

No matter how many children are trapped in the inner recesses of our psyche, it is our task to release them from their respective prisons and the power of the demon(s) that keep them there. As Abel, Lazarus, Dana, Chris and others have claimed back their various inner children, they found the unsound eye was restored to health and they no longer lived in a land of darkness, but in a land of light. They were able to claim what they saw with their eyes and what they heard with their ears. Light penetrated their souls and they were enlivened. The light of their being no longer needed to be hidden from the eyes of the world. Rather, the bushel of the unconscious realm of the psyche could be lifted and the light of the life force could shine before all to see.

PART IV

The Messianic Struggle for the Soul of Humankind

149e

∞14∞
The Power of the IAM

THE MEANING OF THE MIRACLES

For Jesus to jolt us out of the downward spiral of toxic guilt and shame and the intense worthlessness and emptiness that that in turn generates, he had to do more than merely teach a different way of regarding our Selves and others around us. Beyond the teaching, he had to demonstrate that he had power and authority greater than that claimed by the demon. Because the roots of the demon's existence lie in our experience of our parents it seems to possess the power of God: omnipotence (all-powerful), omniscience (all knowing), and omnipresence (always around). To counter the claims of the demonic force, Jesus had to demonstrate that his power of authority came from the true God who is truly omnipotent, omniscient, omnipresent and so all-loving. If he was able to do that, the god-power claimed by the demonic force would be invalidated and rendered empty.

Jesus was able to demonstrate that he possessed incredible power, emanating from within him, by being true to his IAM-ness. It was not a sham-power like that of the demon, which depends upon mirrors and magic tricks. It was, rather, a power that actually changed things; a power that emanated from the pure IAM.

In chapter seven, we examined how the religious leaders who opposed Jesus were metaphors for the demonic force. Jesus demonstrated the authority of his power through his interactions with these men. As the two sides engaged each other, they progressively revealed the source and extent of their power. The demon (in the form of the religious leaders) revealed itself to demand that others believe they needed approval in order to be of value and worth. Jesus, on the other hand, did not need that affirmation. On the contrary, when people began to believe in him because his IAM power was manifest through the miracles, he backed away from the acclaim and wonder with which others responded to him (John 2:23–25; John 5:41). He knew the trap that this contained, namely that people would remain awestruck at the manifestation of his power, rather than understanding what the manifestation meant. If the miracle itself becomes the end, then the demon wins the battle—because dependence on superficial happenings displaces the substantial inner meaning.

Jesus realized this after the multiplication of the loaves and the fishes. Because he did not want to get caught up in that agenda, he retreated from the people's presence, even at the cost of losing many of his followers (John 6:10–15, 53–66). He would not be caught in the trap of needing others' approval to reinforce and affirm who he was. That would place him where every other human person stood, engulfed by the power of darkness. By refuting that need, Jesus struck a debilitating blow to the demon's attempt to control him.

Most of us look to have our goodness validated by others. As a result, the identity of our IAM experience is eroded and corrupted; we play right into the demon's hands and we lose our IAM power. The Prince of Darkness deludes us into believing that our value and worth and therefore the substance of our life comes from the "glory" of others. Jesus was able to avoid this trick of the demon because he knew he did not need anyone to affirm him, because, as the second person of the Godhead, he was firmly rooted in his being, and thus knew he was not in need of the demon's promises of granting worth and value.

THE POWER OF THE UNFRACTURED IAM

Jesus was empowered to concentrate his IAM energy, to do things that the rest of us cannot do, because of the integrity of his IAM. We cannot perform miracles because our IAM power within is splintered and weakened and we are under the demon's control. This is affirmed by Jesus when he says, "If you had faith (in the power of the IAM), you could uproot this tree or move that mountain" (Matt. 17:21; Luke 17:6).

Jesus used his unfractured IAM power when performing miracles to startle us into an acknowledgment of the power of faith so that we might be saved from the demon that strangles and suffocates us from inside. There are several miracles recounted that involve the calming of a violent storm when Jesus' disciples are in a boat in the middle of a large body of water. One of these in particular reveals a number of qualities about the power of the IAM.

After the multiplication of the loaves and fishes, Jesus retreats to the far shore of a large body of water. His disciples, wanting to meet up with him on the other side, get into a boat. On the way, they encounter a great storm. As the storm batters the boat, the disciples see someone walking on the water. They are terrified, and think it is a ghost. Jesus calls out to them not to be afraid. When Peter realizes that it is Jesus, he calls out, asking him if he, too, can come out onto the water. Jesus invites him to do so. Peter climbs out of the boat and begins to walk on the water. But fear overtakes him and he begins to sink. He cries out to Jesus to save him. Jesus reaches out his hand, catches him and says, "Why did you doubt and lose faith?" (Matt. 14:22–33; a similar miracle is recounted in Luke 14:22–23).

Jesus beckons to Peter to exercise the power of his pure, unfractured IAM. Initially, Peter draws on that power and does walk upon the water, demonstrating what power the energy of the IAM generates if it is allowed to remain intact. Reading between the lines, however, we can hear the demon effect the fracture of Peter's IAM integrity: "Come on, Peter! Who are you trying to fool? You haven't got what it takes to butt this wind and walk on water. Watch out! That wave is going to overwhelm you! Be careful! You're not going to make it!"

With that, Peter's IAM-integrity begins to crumble. The original inner energy he was drawing on wanes—and he begins to sink. True power rests in being faithful to God's will as it is found in the IAM-ness which God created in His image and likeness.

Our internal demon brings with it great, violent turmoil when we are under its dominion. This miracle serves as a metaphor for what we must do in the face of the demonic onslaught. If we draw from our IAM power, we can conquer the inner storm and that which causes it. If, however, we give in to its activity, we will sink and drown in the anxiety and turmoil it generates within us.

Part of the problem is that we don't recognize the power that lies within our Selves. Instead of accepting the miracle, the disciples were terrified because they thought they were seeing a ghost. When it is time for us to call upon our inner IAM resource, we too are frightened of it. We dismiss it as not having relevance for us, and as a result, we are at the mercy of the storm within us.

Yet, when we do call on the power of our IAM, our helplessness disappears. Whenever someone in therapy stands up to their demon(s) calling on their IAM power, I ask them if there has been any internal change. The answer always is, "I no longer feel it has power over me. I feel more in control." If there is residual turmoil, this invariably means that some part of the demon's attack has not yet been addressed. When that is done, the inner storm is always calmed. But, again, that requires that we be faithful to our own IAM power through to the conclusion of the battle that may be raging inside. If we don't, we will eventually sink just as Peter did.

THE RADIANCE OF THE IAM

Through another miracle, the Transfiguration, Jesus demonstrates what is in store for us. At one point, Jesus took Peter, James and his brother John to a high mountain where they would be alone. There, he was transfigured before them. His face had the light of the sun and his garments gleamed with a white glow. Then, Moses and Elijah appeared and talked with him. Peter suggested they make three shrines, one each for Jesus, Moses, and Elijah. As he said this, a brilliant light enveloped them and a voice from the cloud said, "This is my beloved son. I am most pleased with him. Listen to him." When the three disciples heard this they were struck down with awe. Then Jesus touched them and told them not to be afraid. And when they looked up, it was only the four of them who were now there (Matt. 17:1–8).

By being faithful to the center of his being, his IAM-ness, Jesus reveals both its purity and the bond with God that resides within it. So he says to us, if we are faithful to our own inner "god-like" image, the light within us will shine like the sun and will manifest itself to us and others. But beyond that, being centered in our birthright, the energy of our IAM will be unfettered, without walls of fear, shame and guilt, and be open to the approach and embrace of our uncreated, creating, nurturing, loving Parent God in the fullness of our being.

∞15∞
<u>Darkness and Light Wrestling</u>

D-Day Approaches

As the tension builds between Jesus, the confident, assertive IAM, and the power hungry, unrelenting demon figures, they become more confrontational and hostile—very much like the kinds of attacks Chris and Dana experienced as they became more aggressive about keeping their integrity within their own IAM centers.

At one point, the dark powers become so incensed with Jesus (because he has progressively challenged their darkness with his light), they begin to take up rocks to stone him. Jesus reminds them of all that he has done to give testimony to his mission. They try to sidestep that reminder by saying it is not his works that they quarrel with, but rather his claim that he is God.

Jesus outmaneuvers them by quoting Scripture, which says all human persons are gods. What harm can there be in him claiming what is true of all humanity to underscore the truth and power of his mission as it is manifest in his works and teachings? He challenges them either to accept what he claims to be his divine mission based on the witness that is given in the miracles and other manifestations of power, or to dismiss him as some kind of quack. And, although he doesn't say it, it is implied that if he is nothing more than a quack, then why are they getting so upset about him? That infuriates them even more. They try to stone him again, but he slips away from them (John 10:31–39).

Stiff-Necked to the Truth

The demon powers are now frantic in their attempts to undermine the authority of his IAM. It is impossible to deny the power that emanates from him in his integrity and wholeness, yet, despite this witness, they refuse to be converted. They want his complete capitulation to them, even if it means they have to kill him. Anything else would mean that they would have to capitulate to him, which would be intolerable. It is to be a battle to the death.

While he is in the temple, they again confront him, accusing him of being an impostor, saying that all the signs that he had performed were not true. Jesus answers simply: "I know who IAM. No matter how hard you want to deny it, that is an inner truth within me. As long as you refuse to see what is in the signs I perform before you, you cannot know who IAM. If you refuse to believe the truth of what you see, then you neither know me nor the One who sent me. If you accept what you see and thereby know me, you also know the One who sent me" (John 8:13–20).

Jesus comes to acknowledge what Chris and Dana and all of us must come to face—the demons will not compromise or listen to reason. They will not let go of any power over the IAM. They are immovable in their position, and hold not one *iota* of respect for the sanctity of the Self. They cannot see or hear beyond their need to rule the IAM with a tyranny that requires the death of Self-awareness. As they reveal their tyranny, we must face them as Jesus did. But there is no need to be flustered by the attacks of the Dark One. Rather, by standing firm in one's own spot, the answer comes from deep inside, and pierces to the core of the demonic heart. We must not worry about being rejected by them; we must reject them instead. Only when we do that can we give them up as our slave masters and become free as we were meant to be.

CONDEMNATION OF THE DEMONIC

"If anyone causes any of these little ones," Jesus says, "to lose faith in the Messiah and his message, that one would be drowned with a great millstone around his neck into the depths of the sea" (Matt. 18:5a–7a). That is what the Inner Demon does: it causes the children of God to lose faith that we are His children and therefore good. The corruption, undermining and devaluing of our IAM-ness is sin. Our IAM-ness is created by God and is in the image and likeness of Him who saw that it was "very good" (Gen. 1:31). To denigrate the IAM and make a person believe otherwise about him- or herself is to blaspheme God in His works. Thus, any agent who is responsible for this is an enemy of God. In Jesus' eyes then, any such power deserves the worst of punishments, one from which there is no escape.

Jesus tells two stories to some Pharisees that point up the guilt of their system (Matt. 21:28–41):

The first story tells of two sons who are asked by their father to do some work for him. The first says he will work, but does not. The second refuses his father, but then repents and does go to work.

The second is the story of a powerful landowner who plants a vineyard, hires attendants, leaves the vineyard in their stead and goes away. When he wants to receive the fruit of his vineyard, he sends his servants to collect. But they are beaten and murdered. Then he sends his son who also is murdered. The landowner then has no choice but to come and destroy the attendants, and give the vineyard to others to look after for him.

After each story, the leaders are asked what they think of the actions of the characters. They proclaim the first son unfaithful and the hirelings criminals.

On saying this, they pronounce the sentence of guilt upon themselves, for they too (like the first son) have promised to do the work of God and have not done it; they too (like the hired attendants) have beaten and killed those who would come to collect the true fruits of the relationship with God. They have blocked the truth of who God is, and have constructed a God of shame and guilt.

THE SHOWDOWN

The religious leaders remain unmoved in their refusal to hear and see the significance of the signs Jesus has given to them so that they may be converted from their darkness to his light. They gather together to plot his death. As they argue and debate among themselves about what they should do, they find themselves in a bind. If they allow him his freedom, the people will hold him up to be a prophet. They fear this will arouse the Romans to attack the nation and destroy it. The High Priest tells them that Jesus must die if the nation is to be saved. They all agree and begin to plot how they are going to go about doing it (John 11:47–53).

But even as they are plotting, they reveal themselves. There has been no indication that the Romans are in the least threatened by this man. The threat is all a construction of their minds; a product of their futurizing and mind reading. This results in distorted and fabricated data upon which they based their decision to murder Jesus.

PREPARING FOR THE FINAL ONSLAUGHT

As the powers of darkness are plotting Jesus' death, he is preparing for it himself. After the Passover meal, he reassures the disciples that the love of the God-Parent and their own integrity will see them through this dark period. He goes into the Garden of Gethsemane where the fear, distress, and sorrow of his ordeal overtake him. He finds himself terribly alone, for even his closest friends have fallen into a deep sleep. So added to his pain is an absolute sense of loneliness and abandonment. However, once he has expressed and faced his pain, he is released from it so that he may consummate his mission.

As clients come ever closer to rejecting the way of life as it had been dictated to them by their demons, the threats of death intensify. They begin to experience a deepening of the loneliness and depression that seemed to have abated earlier in their journeys. Old somatic symptoms intensify to levels that seem to exceed the ones that were present when they came into the counseling process. New ones appear with a vengeance. And they hear the demons jeering at them, saying, "You haven't gotten anywhere with this therapy stuff! See how much you hurt all over, how anxious you are! Ha! Ha! Ha!"

With all of this, clients began to falter in their resolve. "Can Jack be right? If it hurts this much, am I really hurting my Self by going through all of this? Is it worth it?" Now comes the time for them to make the leap of faith or to give in to the powers of darkness within their Selves. From their vantage point, it looks as though they're on the edge of a precipice, looking down into a bottomless void. On the opposite edge, I am saying, "Take the leap. I know it looks like a great canyon, wide and deep, but it is no larger than a crack in the sidewalk." Their demons keep reminding them how far apart the canyon ledges are and how bottomless the pit. Making the leap appears to be leading to total destruction.

Anyone who enters into this inner struggle will have to come to the point of profound fear and despair. It will seem to us as though there is no one to be with us while we enter into this place of utter darkness. But since Jesus, the divine representative, chose to enter into this same place, we know that we have a companion in the depth of that darkness who stands with us in that desolate space.

BRUTALIZING THE TRUTH

We now see the cruelty that is visited upon those who refuse to give in to the demons and instead holds fast to their IAM integrity: The men holding Jesus mock and beat him; they blindfold him and shout, "Prophesy! Who is it who is hitting you?" Then the High Priest questions him. Jesus objects that he has done nothing in secret, everyone has seen and heard everything he has done and said. One of the soldiers strikes him and asks him if that is any way to speak to the High Priest. Jesus then says, "If I am lying, then tell me what the lie is; otherwise, if I have spoken the truth, why am I being punished?" (John 18:19–24). It is clear that the demon powers punish us for telling the truth, just as the religious leaders punished Jesus.

THE CONFUSED AND OVERWHELMED CENTRAL I

The soldiers and the religious leaders then take Jesus to the Roman governor Pilate. In three successive encounters with them, he challenges the charges they bring against Jesus. Their charges remain unclear. After each challenge, Pilate takes Jesus aside and questions him, and each time he is convinced that Jesus has done no wrong. In the final encounter with Jesus, Pilate asks him, "Where are you from?" No answer. "Don't you know that I have the power to either free you or give you the death penalty? I think it might be a good idea if you answered my questions." Jesus answers, "You really don't. All this is happening because it is ordained from above. The ones who are sinning are those who delivered me to you."

It is clear that Pilate is reluctant to kill Jesus. So whom does he represent in this mythological struggle?

As this passion unfolds, Jesus represents the part of our Selves that resides at the very core of our IAM-ness, the part that will not compromise any of our integrity. It is the part of our Self who is our deepest truth but who, under the dominion of the Prince of Darkness, is buried deep inside by it and is trying to murder this persona of truth. This is the part of the Self that Jesus, as the Incarnate God, has come to honor and help us reclaim.

Pilate is clearly not a member of the party of darkness who is trying to destroy the light of integrity. He is baffled and confused by what is going on. He seems to understand what is happening but is unable to stand up for what he believes: that this person who is standing before him is not guilty as charged.

These are the qualities displayed by the Central I, buffeted about by forces inside the psyche that influence it in its decision-making process. Because it is confused and overwhelmed by demonic attacks, it too enters, by default, into the abuse directed at the truth part of the Self. This is the character of Pilate.

Jesus' statement to Pilate—that he does not have the power of life and death over him, but that what will happen has been ordained from above—has several layers of meaning. The first of these is that in the core of the truth of the Self, no one, not even the Central I, has the power to destroy it. The second level of meaning is that what will happen needs to happen. Jesus needs to follow through with his struggle to the bitter end in order for his mission to be completed.

CAVING IN TO THE POWER OF DARKNESS

Convinced of Jesus' innocence, Pilate goes out once again and tries to release him. But the crowd says that if he does that he betrays Caesar, for this man claims to be a king and there can only be one king—and that is Caesar! This is something that Pilate cannot allow, for it could bring about a dreaded uprising. He decides he must bring this scene to a close, and sits down on the judgment seat to indicate that a decision is going to be made. He tries one last maneuver to see if he can get them to back off. So he says, "Here is your king!" They persist, "Crucify him!" "Shall I execute your king?" he asks. But even that backfires for they retort, "We have no king but Caesar!"

Pilate gets their point. "If I don't get rid of this man, regardless of whether he is innocent or not, I'm going to look like a traitor to Caesar and I can't stand up to that." He hands Jesus over to be crucified and they lead him away (John 19:5–16).

When the Allies of Demons are at a frenzied pitch like this, the Central I becomes intimidated by them, capitulates and abandons its core of integrity to them. The Central I has the power to prevent the crucifixion of integrity. However, when that action *appears* to be a betrayal of the Inner Other (Caesar), the Central I will choose to capitulate. A modern day example might be: John Doe is a plant supervisor. A worker comes to him and complains that Sam, another man on the line, wants to do things his own way. The supervisor says, "I don't see what the problem is. Sam hasn't done anything wrong." But the first worker says, "If you don't fire that man, we'll tell the CEO you're not following the rules, and you'll lose *your* job." The supervisor, afraid of boss, goes against his own better judgment and fires Sam.

THE POWER OF DARKNESS BEGINS TO CRUMBLE

The soldiers take Jesus and force him to carry his own cross to the place called the Skull. There they crucify him (John 19:17–18). But this is not the end of the story. When they get out to the Skull, they find that Pilate has written an inscription to be placed on the cross with Jesus that reads, "This is Jesus of Nazareth, the King of the Jews." When the religious leaders read this, they rush back to Pilate and object. They want him to have it rewritten to say, "This man says, 'I am the King of the Jews.'" But Pilate responds, "This is what I have written and that's the way it is" (John 19:19–22).

So even though the Central I has been maneuvered into giving over the core of integrity to the dark force, he does not leave him completely abandoned. Pilate's inscription confirms that the person they are putting to death, the IAM, *is* the king. In other words, the Central I knows that the place of truth is the place of power and is the king of the Self—even though he cannot bring himself to stop the crucifixion. The dark forces are beginning to lose their grip on the situation.

Now the time arrives to see who will be the victor. During the three hours that he hangs there, a great darkness covers the land. At the end, Jesus cries out, "My God, My God, why have you abandoned me?" Then there is a loud groan, the death groan, and he gives up his spirit (Matt. 27:45–47).

There is this same sense of utter despair and abandonment for any of us as we enter fully into this inner process of freeing our Selves from the chains of our demons. It seems as though the whole world implodes upon us when we reach this point in the final battle with the powers of darkness. It certainly seems as though we have entered the realm of the dead where all that is familiar is gone, where the core of existence seems to be in a state of limbo. When Jesus dies, it seems as though the power of darkness has won in the last round. But has God really forsaken Jesus?

At the moment of his death the earth begins to rumble and shake, rocks are split open, the veil in the temple is rent in two, tombs open and many who were asleep in death come alive (Matt. 27:51–53). So even as he dies, there is great energy and a contradiction that portends the possibility that the dark forces are not winning this war with the light.

DEATH TO THE POWERS OF DARKNESS

Jesus is laid to rest. A stone is rolled over the opening to seal the tomb. Night falls, the Sabbath begins and the quiet of the holy time sets into the countryside.

Once any person who has fought the hardest of battles passes through that place of "death," there is an unfamiliar sense of calm and quiet. Everything is strange. It is like having gone through a tremendous storm; there are limbs of trees and other debris strewn everywhere. But everything seems to be clean. There is a smell of freshness in the air, and everything seems enveloped in a shroud of quiet.

What this death quiet symbolizes is not only the murder of truth and integrity of the Self, but also the death of the Self to the dark forces. Initially, our demons tell us, "If you stop listening to us, you will die." As we go through the therapeutic process and begin to question these demon voices, their threats become stronger. "If you stop listening to us, we will kill you." But in the end, the "you" they kill is not the real, core "you." It is the demon-powered you. When this threat is carried out, it is, paradoxically, the demon who "dies." We are freed, and that is our resurrection.

RESURRECTION FROM THE DEATH OF THE DARK POWER

After the burial, the sun sets on the Sabbath and the Holy Day is officially over. The next morning, Jesus' loved ones will be able to visit the sepulcher and finish the burial procedure. As soon as light begins to show on the horizon, Mary Magdalene and the other Mary hurry off to the place of entombment.

When they arrive, there is a great rumble like an earthquake, and the Marys see that the stone has been rolled back. Sitting on the stone is an angel of the Lord who is as bright as lightning, his robes white as new fallen snow.

The angel says to the women, "Don't be afraid. I know you are looking for Jesus who was crucified. He is not here. He has risen from the dead as he said he would. Come see." They look in and see that Jesus is not there. The angel then instructs them to go tell the rest of the disciples that Jesus is risen. They rush off filled with excitement, fear and joy to tell the rest what has come to be. On their way, they meet Jesus. He greets them and they fall down before him, hugging his feet. He tells them not to be afraid and to tell the rest that he is alive (Matt. 28:1–10). Jesus has risen into new life, victorious over the darkness.

THE RESURRECTION TIME

After the resurrection, Jesus appeared to the disciples over a period of forty days. Luke's account (chap. 24) of the time of the resurrection centers around Jesus reminding his followers that it was foretold that the Messiah must suffer at the hands of sinful people and die, then rise from the dead on the third day after his death. Jesus' followers are so focused on the victory of the powers of darkness they forgot and, as a result, could not believe that Jesus was ultimately victorious over those forces. The disciples have difficulty hearing the message of victory, just as we have difficulty believing that we will pass through our difficulties and be victorious. No matter how much we might falter in our battle against the

Evil One, if we are essentially faithful to the Power of Light, we will be heirs to the victory of the resurrection.

THE ASCENSION

When forty days have gone by, Jesus directs his disciples to teach and baptize in his name. He then reassures them that he will be with them for all time. With that, he raises up his arms in blessing and ascends into the heavens.

Because his IAM identity flowed from the Source IAM and was not a created IAM, it was not possible that his IAM integrity could in any way be jeopardized. Therefore, even though he was tempted by the Inner Other Demons as we all are—and with the same temptations—he did not fall before them. That does not mean he did not endure the effects of the power of the Satanic, inner power. Clearly he did. He wrestled with it at the end of his fasting sojourn in the desert. He suffered its evil power in his engagements with the religious leaders who opposed the message of God that Jesus represented. It was the power of the Inner Other that betrayed him, flogged and scorned him, placed a crown of thorns on his head and ultimately crucified him.

But because he never compromised the integrity of his IAM, he remains intact as a human being. After death, he is not separated in body and soul but remains totally integrated. Thus, in the final act of his life as the man-God Jesus, he shows us how important being faithful to our integrity is.

THE FINAL VICTORY

The war for the soul of humankind has been won by the power of the IAM, the power of light. The powers of darkness have lost the war forever. They have lost the power to enslave the soul of humankind in the name of God. Their ultimate weapon, to speak in the name of God, has been revealed by the Son of God for what it is: a terrible deception that has bound the heart of humankind. Not only has the deception been revealed, but their power has been proved to be illusory. Rising from the dead, Jesus demonstrated that to be true to the IAM is the power by which the forces of darkness will be dethroned and cast into the everlasting fire. It is not Jesus who died that day, it is they who died because of their misuse of the word of God and their abuse of God's power.

Through Jesus, God demonstrated that He is not on their side. Quite to the contrary, God is their committed adversary.

∞16∞
Our Journey

THE INTIMACY OF THE INCARNATION

As we come into an awareness of and wage our own version of the cosmic war with the power of darkness, we do so knowing that God is with us, and that His Son has entered into the dark place with the same trepidation we feel. Jesus' life demonstrates the firmness of the God-Parent's love for us. He bestowed upon us His own Son to bear witness to His presence in our battle and to offer us concrete assistance by personally waging the war against the power of darkness—and demonstrating that if we are faithful to the light, victory will be ours.

When the Son of God died on the cross, the Evil One appeared momentarily to be right, powerful and victorious. It was only a moment. After three days, Jesus rose in the glorious light of new life. With that event as the new backdrop, the words he spoke earlier appear in a new light: If a person is to enter the Kingdom of God, he or she has to be reborn in the Spirit. That which is of the flesh is flesh. That which is of the Spirit is spirit (John 3:3–6).

Paul echoes this when he writes (in Rom. 6:5–7) that when a Christian is baptized, he or she is united with Christ, and will therefore certainly be united with him in the resurrection. The old Self (the part of the Self that is the ally and slave to the demon force within) is crucified with him.

THE COSMIC WAR IS OVER

Through the resurrection and the ascension, the cosmic war is over. Our individual wars are not, however. The Prince of Darkness continues to work at entrapping the minds, hearts and souls of humankind. This is underscored in the final chapter of Matthew. There, it is reported that the guards who had been frightened out of their wits with the appearance of angels and an empty tomb return to the city to inform the religious leaders what had happened. They tell the soldiers to spread the story that Jesus' disciples have taken his body away in secret while they were asleep to "make it appear that he had risen as he had foretold." They assure the guards that if Pilate should hear of this, he will not punish them for dereliction of duty because they will persuade him otherwise (Matt. 28:11–15).

This demonstrates that the powers of darkness will continue to lie, deceive and manipulate even after the power of light has been victorious through the resurrection. Those lies, deceits and manipulations are against us who still struggle with our own personal manifestation of the war with the cosmic darkness.

WE ARE IN THE WORLD

Recognizing that we still have our own war in front of us and that the war takes place within the context of the world within which we live, Jesus utters the following prayer: "I do not pray for the world but for those who hear what I have come to say. I am no longer in the world, but they are. I pray to you, Father, that you keep them safe in your name. I have been faithful to them. None has been lost except the one who did what he had to do, the son of sin. I have given them what you sent me for. And the world hates them because of it. *I do not pray that you take them out of the world* but that you keep them from the Evil One. They are not of the world as I am not. Keep them in the truth so that they may be holy. As you have sent me into the world, so I send them there also. I pray not just for these but for all who believe because of their witness. The glory of the truth which you have given to me, I now give to them. The world does not know you, Father. But I have known you and these have known you through me. And now the love that has been yours for me will be in them" (John 17:9–26).

Even though he pledges his constancy to us, he makes it clear that we are to remain in the world. That is, we will exist in time and space, and in an environment, both internal and external, where we will be buffeted about by currents and whirlwinds created by the power of darkness.

THE NEW CREATION

Because of that complete involvement in our life and struggle, the opening hymn of the New Creation in the Gospel of St. John is proclaimed:

> In the beginning the Word was and the Word was with
> God, and the Word was God. He was in the beginning

> with God. All things were made through him, and with-
> out him nothing was made that came into existence.
> Through him life came to be, and that life was the light
> of human kind. This light shines in the darkness, and
> the darkness has not overcome it . . . This true light that
> enlightens everyone was coming into the world. He was
> in the world, the world was made through him, yet the
> world knew him not. He came to his own home, and
> his own people received him not. But to all who received
> him, who believed in his name he gave power to become
> children of God; who were born, not out of the natur-
> al world or any human drive or the will of anyone, but
> of God. So the Word became flesh and lived among us
> for a time, and we witnessed the fullness of grace bestowed
> upon him by the Holy One . . . From the fullness of his
> grace we all share his blessing . . . Behold the Lamb of
> God, who takes away the sin of the world (John 1: 1–5,
> 9–14,16, 30).

This is not the story of the creation of the physical world out of chaos, darkness and void as it is recounted in Genesis 1; rather, it is the story of the creation of the new spiritual world of light out of the unworld-ly chaos, darkness and void. Unlike the first creation account in Gene-sis in which Adam and Eve were passive participants in their creation, the Adam and Eve of the new spiritual creation are very active in their regeneration: "But to all who received him . . . he gave power to become children of God." The new Adam and Eve have an active voice in the spiritual re-creation by choosing to receive the Word. Those who choose to receive the Word are choosing to be restored in fullness of the chil-dren of God.

Jesus was the light that came to dispel the darkness of the spiritual chaos spawned by our Inner Demons. Jesus, as the Word, entered fully into our human nature. Everything that was ours was his, except the rift of toxic shame and guilt that is between God and our Selves.

BEING DELIVERED UP TO THE POWERS OF DARKNESS

Our eyes have been opened to the possibility of light in the land of dark-ness. As we carry on the struggle not to be overcome by the darkness, Jesus tells us we will be delivered up to and flogged by all kinds of powers (as he was) for not giving up the truth and not capitulating to them.

As we try to cope with that struggle against the darkness, he tells us not to be worried about what our response will be. Rather, we should allow what will happen *to* happen. When it does happen, the Spirit will be with us and the Creator will speak through us if we have faith in the moment.

The array of powers that will hate us because we refuse to deny the truth will be enormous. It will range from great powers of state to potent powers within the household—father against son, mother against daughter, brother against brother. But have no fear. The truth will prevail. For what has been said in darkness will now be proclaimed in the light. Be assured that God values us very highly. If we are constant in our faith to the truth that is within us, we will be saved (Matt. 10:17–30).

THE BATTERED SELF SYNDROME

Even though our eyes have been opened to the powers of darkness, even though we are beaten up unmercifully by them, we tenaciously embrace them. This certainly interrupts our ability to part from them and to follow the light of the Christ. What causes us to cling to them so?

1. We believe that we cannot function without them. We think we will founder in life without their guidance, and will ultimately die in helplessness.

2. At the same time, we don't believe in their existence. If we refuse to believe that they exist, then we will not be able to own what they do to us and take action against them. This disbelief is spawned by the demon itself. Its reasoning works this way: "How silly to believe that I'm real. What will people think of you if they find out you believe you have demons? I'll tell you what they'll think. They will think you're crazy—that's what they'll think!" The irony, of course, is that even as the demon is in the process of dissuading us from acknowledging and confronting its existence, it is revealing itself.

3. Because the internal demons were created by our Selves in response to our experience of our parents, we confuse the two. Thus, if we allow our Selves to feel anger and hatred for the demon force inside our Selves, we believe that anger and hatred is for our true, flesh-and-blood parents, and we fear that will destroy the bond of love between us.

4. When we fashioned our internal images of our parents in the person of the Inner Other, we gave it the same absolute power over us that we experienced our external parents having over us. Thus, when we challenge its power, we are like children standing before our parents in a position of *perceived* inferiority. So when we challenge its present authority over us and we get a response such as "You're not powerful enough to get rid of me, so just don't try," we are intimidated and we run away.

5. When we challenge our demons' authority over us, they threaten us with death as they did Jesus. Because of the original circumstances under which they were created, it appears to us as though they do have that power over us. However, in response to that Jesus says: "Whosoever loves father or mother, son or daughter more than me, is not worthy of me. Whosoever does not enter into the struggle of the cross that I have born is not worthy of me. Whosoever looks to save his life will lose it; anyone who dies for my sake will live" (Matt. 10:37–39).

THE THREAT OF DEATH

It is important to remember that the Inner Other Demon is a persona not a person. It is a force that exists inside of our psyche only because we give it existence and, unlike our Selves, is not self-aware. It does not have feelings, thoughts or perceptions of its own.

Anything it says or does is a result of the way that we programmed it. It is like an internal robot that, when set off by specific stimuli, reacts in predetermined ways. It appears to have a will of its own, but that is only appearance.

However, it is an internal object with which *we* have a very intense cognitive, emotional and psychological relationship. When we engage it, it appears to respond as though it is an independent person. But it is not. The appearance of being a person with an independent internal life is a part of its program.

Thus, when we begin to challenge its authority over us, it is programmed to resist. Its ensuing attacks appear to us to be life threatening. We believe it holds the power of life and death in its hands because it reacts in the same way a real person who is invested in and threatened by a challenge to its authority would react.

If we are to be victorious over these powers, we must convert those inner parts of our Selves to believe the message the Messiah delivered to the Evil One: "You make a tree rotten and you make what it bears to be rotten also. You are a brood of poisonous snakes! How can what you say be good when you are evil? I condemn you because through your words you bring evil into the world" (Matt. 12:33–37). If we can do that, we too will discover and reclaim in that deep inner place our birthright as the unadulterated children of God.

If we are to be free, we too must face and experience the same death that Jesus underwent. If we attempt to avoid that, Jesus warns us: "The gate that is broad and easy leads to destruction. And many take it, thinking it leads to life. But don't be fooled. Take, rather, the narrow gate, for although the way is hard, it leads to life" (Matt. 7:13–14).

THE FRUITS OF GOING AGAINST THE FLOW

Those who go against the temptation of the Dark One and follow Jesus, the Christ, choose to go against the flow of life as it is accepted and practiced by the world at large—the world that is conditioned by the Inner Other Power, the world of darkness. There is, therefore, pain that is great at times, but Jesus assures us: "Blessed are you the poor, for yours is the kingdom of God. And you that hunger shall be satisfied. And you who weep shall laugh. And blessed are you whom the power of Darkness hates and reviles and labels your name as evil on account of your faithfulness to what I preach and stand for. Rejoice and leap for joy for behold your reward is great!" (Luke 6:20–23).

Once we have made that leap, the power of the IAM will be at our disposal. Once we have claimed our inheritance as gods in the image and likeness of the one God, we will come to understand what Jesus meant when he said, "Come to me, all you who are heavy burdened, and I will give you rest. If you take upon your Self my yoke, you will find it to be light and you will find rest in your souls" (Matt. 11:28–30).

INVESTING IN THE GIFTS OF THE SELF

If we live entirely for our Selves, we will violate others and become enclosed upon our Selves. But unless we take that risk in responding to our own life energies, we will not experience our own inner sense of life. If we do not take that risk, we cannot realize and acknowledge that there are others who have the same kind of inner experience of living energy that we do, and who have the same right to experience it as we do. If we are always worried about others, if we do not pay attention to this "inner aliveness" that is the primary gift of our Creator God for fear that it will alienate us from others, we become dead to our Selves and to one another.

To illustrate the need to invest in life, Jesus tells the story of three servants who are given money by their master to invest while he is away on a long trip. When he returns, he calls the three to give an accounting. The first two tell him that they have invested his money and have doubled its value. The master is pleased and says to both, "You have done well. I commend you. Because you have worked with the resource I gave you, and even taken some risks with it, I reward you with authority over my cities."

The third servant, however, says, "I was afraid of you and fearful that you might punish me severely if I lost any of that which you gave me. So I hid it away to wait for your return. So here is your one pound."

The lord becomes very angry and says to this servant, "You knew that I expected yield from my resource. The least you could have done was put it in the bank so it would have collected interest. Take the pound from him and give it to the one who earned ten! I say to you all, whoever works with what I give them will be given more. Those who don't, what little they have will be taken away from them" (Luke 19:11–26).

The message is clear. Those who invest and work with what they have been given by the Creator will reap dividends in life energy and fulfill the will of the Holy One. Those who listen to the demon force and squelch their life force for fear they will offend the powers-that-be will lose what they have been given.

WE ARE NOT TO BE WORRY WARTS

Jesus' intent is not to transform us into worry warts about our salvation, always wondering and anxious about whether we do the "right thing" or not. That would have made him like the people who put him to death. Jesus truly loves us. His primary concern is to help us free our Selves from the clutches of the Evil One and light the way along the path of personal integrity and inner truth. As the Word, he realizes that this is the core of our existence. Bringing this to life and fruition is what gives us substance and purpose in life.

Therefore, his message is not a well-defined succession of dos and don'ts. Rather, his life and his teachings offer us new ways of looking at reality that are not distorted by the activity of the Inner Other Demons. The story of the prodigal son presents us with one of those new views.

There was a man who had two sons. The younger of them decided it was time to experience the world beyond the family. So he asked his father for his inheritance. The father gave it to him and the son left, exploring far away lands where he squandered his inheritance. The day finally came when he ran out of money. The only job he could find was to feed the swine of a local farmer. After some time at that and eating more poorly than the swine, he realized that his father's servants fared better than he. So he decided to return home.

When he arrived there, his father ran to him and welcomed, embraced, and kissed him. The son said to him, "Father, I have sinned against you. I am not worthy to be called your son."

But the father responded by instructing the servants to bring the best robe to put on the son; to place a ring on his finger and shoes on his feet; and to kill the fatted calf so that there could be a party to celebrate his son's "return from the dead."

When his older son found out that his brother had returned and how his father had received him, he was very angry and refused to enter the house. The father went out to see if he could coax his son to join in the rejoicing. But the elder son responded, "All these years I have served you and I have never disobeyed you. Yet, you never once gave me a kid, let alone a fatted calf that I might have a party with my friends. Yet when that good-for-nothing son of yours decides he's going to come home, you welcome him with open arms and throw a big party for him—killing the fatted calf!"

The father responded, "Don't you know that we are always together and that all that I have is yours? But your brother, who was lost to me, has returned and I am happy about that. I wanted to throw a party to celebrate that he has come back to us" (Luke 15:11–32).

The prodigal son was certainly not one who was constantly looking over his shoulder, wondering what people were thinking of him and how they might judge him. He opted for the surge of life within him. He made some mistakes, some serious ones: he lived a dissolute life and squandered his inheritance, and his actions caused his father great sadness and worry. It is clear from the story, however, that the mistakes he made were not irremediable.

Quite the contrary, we can sense the intensity of feeling that flowed between this son and his father because of this young man's chutzpah, energy, spontaneity, resourcefulness, aliveness, dynamism, and autonomy. It is precisely because he had those traits and lived in them that he was able to acknowledge the wrong that he had done and repent before his father. But in addition there is an exciting dynamism about him.

And then there was the older brother—the one who fulfilled all of his father's "expectations." He did all that he thought was required of him to *earn* his father's love. He gave up himself so that his father would love him. But he was dull and full of resentment. There was little energy there. There seems to be a deep sadness in the father as he tries to relate to this son.

We can only conclude that his feelings toward the returned son compared to the other are due to the exuberant aliveness of the one as compared to the dutiful lifelessness of the other. The one is full; the other empty.

And that is what Jesus is saying to us. It is more important that we live our lives, taking chances—chances of making mistakes, even of sinning—than to live within the tightness of what we think are others' expectations. To do so drains the life from us. Life in God involves taking risks because, as human beings, the only resource we have to work with is our life energy, and how that manifests itself in our feelings, perceptions, needs, wants and desires.

In the story of the prodigal son, we can sense the shadow of the demon hovering over the stay-at-home brother, always admonishing carefulness, timidity, and restrictiveness in response to life. This jealous brother is an image for the Child-Allied-with-the-Inner-Other. Because of the alliance, that part of the Self mirrors the agenda of the Inner Other. It never gives in, admits a mistake, softens in love or understanding. It is a hard and unyielding persona who will not be convinced beyond its stated position.

As the father tries to convince the son of the wonderful thing that has happened in the return of his brother, he gets no response. We are left with an image of a very jealous and resentful person. There is no reason to believe the elder brother shifted out of that emotional state. When, because of our demons, we live in terror of making a mistake, we also live in bitterness and resentment.

SUCCESS IS NOT THE POINT

Because one of the main pieces of artillery in the demon's war against us is the threat and humiliation of failure, we need to make sure that we don't succumb to its trap in our very attempts to get out from under its heavy weight. We may not always even be aware of the demon's ploys. Because the demon works out of the unconscious, it is often unknown to us. With that in mind, it needs to be pointed out that what counts is not that we successfully claim the fullness of our identity all the time under all circumstances as we struggle to resist the demon's power, but that we move toward awareness, knowing when we are "missing the mark" because of the demonic activity, and *when* we discover that we have unwittingly been taken over by the Evil Force, to exorcise our Selves of it and claim back our true Selves.

That fact that we lose various battles and skirmishes in this personal war we all have is not what brings us damnation. What brings us damnation is losing heart and giving up faith and trust in our birthright.

Jesus assures us that if we hold fast and have courage, we need not fear, as the truth will uncover all that is hidden. What has been told in the dark will be spoken aloud in the light; what has been whispered will be shouted from the housetops. The truth will be revealed in the faithfulness to the struggle, and the goodness of the Self in integrity will shine forth.

THE GIVING OF THE SPIRIT

In addition to everything else Jesus has done for us and the covenant he has made with the Father to protect us in the world in which we find our Selves, he also promises for us a constant companion, the Counselor, the Holy Spirit of Truth, who will be sent in his name (John 14:26). Some of the characteristics of the Spirit are Counselor, Caretaker, Spiritual Nurturer, Wisdom, Quiet Presence. Because those are qualities that are usually associated with the feminine, I see the Holy Spirit as the feminine aspect of the Godhead. Therefore, I refer to the Holy Spirit as "She."

When Jesus promises us the coming of the Holy Spirit, he tells us the Spirit will be sent for a double purpose, the first of which is to aid us on our moment-to-moment struggle with the Evil One:

> And when She comes, She will convince the world concerning sin and righteousness and judgment: concerning sin, because they do not believe in me; concerning righteousness, because I go to the Father, and you will see me no more; concerning judgment, because the ruler of this world is judged (John 16:8–11).

So not only is the world of the Dark One vanquished by the risen Christ, but its world will be continually challenged and condemned by the presence of the Spirit in the community of believers in the true, revealed God of the I AM WHO AM.

Because of the presence of the Spirit, the failure to believe in the Word of God will become most apparent. The presence of the Spirit within the members of the body of the church will constantly show through the witness of living in the light of Christ. To live otherwise is to miss the point of human existence. Because the world insists on living the lie, it is found guilty of choosing to miss the point.

Furthermore, because of the resurrection, Jesus will be taken in fullness to the Father, which proves who was righteous and who possessed the truth.

Finally, the world of darkness, convicted of sin, will stand condemned of holding on to the way of sin and living according to the Law of Appearances rather the Law of the IAM. And that sentence upon the world of darkness will be made manifest by the life that emanates from the community of the Spirit living in the light.

The Holy Spirit, who will be our constant guide and companion, will help us give the witness that will expose the world of darkness for what it is. Because the Counselor dwells within us, the "power of the world cannot know Her" (John 14:16–17). The world is invested in seeing what is on the outside, and therefore cannot know who we are on the inside, where the Spirit dwells.

The second commission of the Mother-Spirit is to provide a context of spiritual safety for us. As he is giving us the Spirit, Jesus tells us not to be troubled or afraid, but rather to abide in the peace he gives to us—not the peace of the world, but a profound peace of the soul (John 14:15–27). The Spirit is bestowed upon us in a context of peace, sent to preserve what Jesus has bestowed. That peace is possible because the Spirit is the power of truth that frees us from the mastery and lies of the Dark One.

It is through the Spirit, who dwells with and in us, that we will continue to experience Jesus' life among us. Thus we are not left orphans in our struggle against the darkness within and without. We have a Savior who was not ruled by the Dark One; a Messiah who wrestled with it unto death but rose in radiant new life to be a witness to the victory we all could enjoy. In addition, in that victory he bestowed upon us the Third Person of the Godhead, the Mother-Counselor-Nurturer-Spirit of Truth to be our constant companion.

KNOWING GOD IN THE IAM

Once released from the power of the Evil One, we are free to exist within our birthright as the imaged likeness of the uncreated IAM, to be in intimate contact with the uncreated consciousness. The Spirit is given to us at Jesus' bequest to aid us in moving toward that intimacy and the possibility of the free flow of the IAM energy between our Selves and God.

Communion with the Mother Spirit brings us to the place in which created IAM meets the Uncreated Consciousness, a state of the pure experience of YHWH that transcends words, thoughts or feelings. It is the spiritual place where we, as the created I AM WHO AM, experience YHWH as She knows us—fully, to the very depth and breadth of our beings. At the same time, we know YHWH as fully as we know our Selves. The only limit to our knowledge of God is the limit of our own being.

It is for this union with YHWH that Jesus came to make war with the power of darkness that dwells within us. Jesus suffered and died at its hands so that at his resurrection, the Dark One's power over us would be destroyed. The resurrection was the fulfillment of Jesus' mission on earth; after that he needed to return to the Father.

But the Mother-Spirit keeps the presence of the power of the God-head with us. She offers us through her presence the possibility of profound intimacy with the Holy One; she illuminates our path as we step out of the shadow of the Dark One and look into the face of the glorious light.